The Reunification of Germany

The Reunification of Germany

by Diane Yancey

WORLD IN CONFLICT

LUCENT Overview Series

Library of Congress Cataloging-in-Publication Data

Yancey, Diane.
   The reunification of Germany / by Diane Yancey.
      p.   cm. — (Lucent overview series)
   Includes bibliographical references and index.
   Summary: Discusses the economic, political, and social impact
of the reunification of Germany.
   ISBN 1-56006-143-X (alk. paper)
   1. Germany—Economic conditions—1990- —Juvenile
literature.   2. Germany—Politics and government—1990- —
Juvenile literature.   3. Germany—Social conditions—1990- —
Juvenile literature.   4. Germany—History—Unification, 1990—
Juvenile literature.   [1. Germany—History—Unification, 1990.]
I. Title.   Series.
HC286.8.Y27   1994
943.087'9—dc20   93-17836
                                                                CIP
                                                                 AC

Copyright © 1994 by Lucent Books, Inc.
P.O. Box 289011, San Diego, CA 92198-9011
Printed in the U.S.A.

16.95

Contents

INTRODUCTION 7

CHAPTER ONE 11
East Versus West

CHAPTER TWO 27
Freedom!

CHAPTER THREE 41
Unification: Dream or Nightmare?

CHAPTER FOUR 55
The Price of Unity

CHAPTER FIVE 71
New Policies, Old Fears

CHAPTER SIX 87
The Invisible Wall

CHAPTER SEVEN 105
A New Germany: Finishing the Work

GLOSSARY 116
SUGGESTIONS FOR FURTHER READING 119
WORKS CONSULTED 120
INDEX 124
ABOUT THE AUTHOR 128
PICTURE CREDITS 128

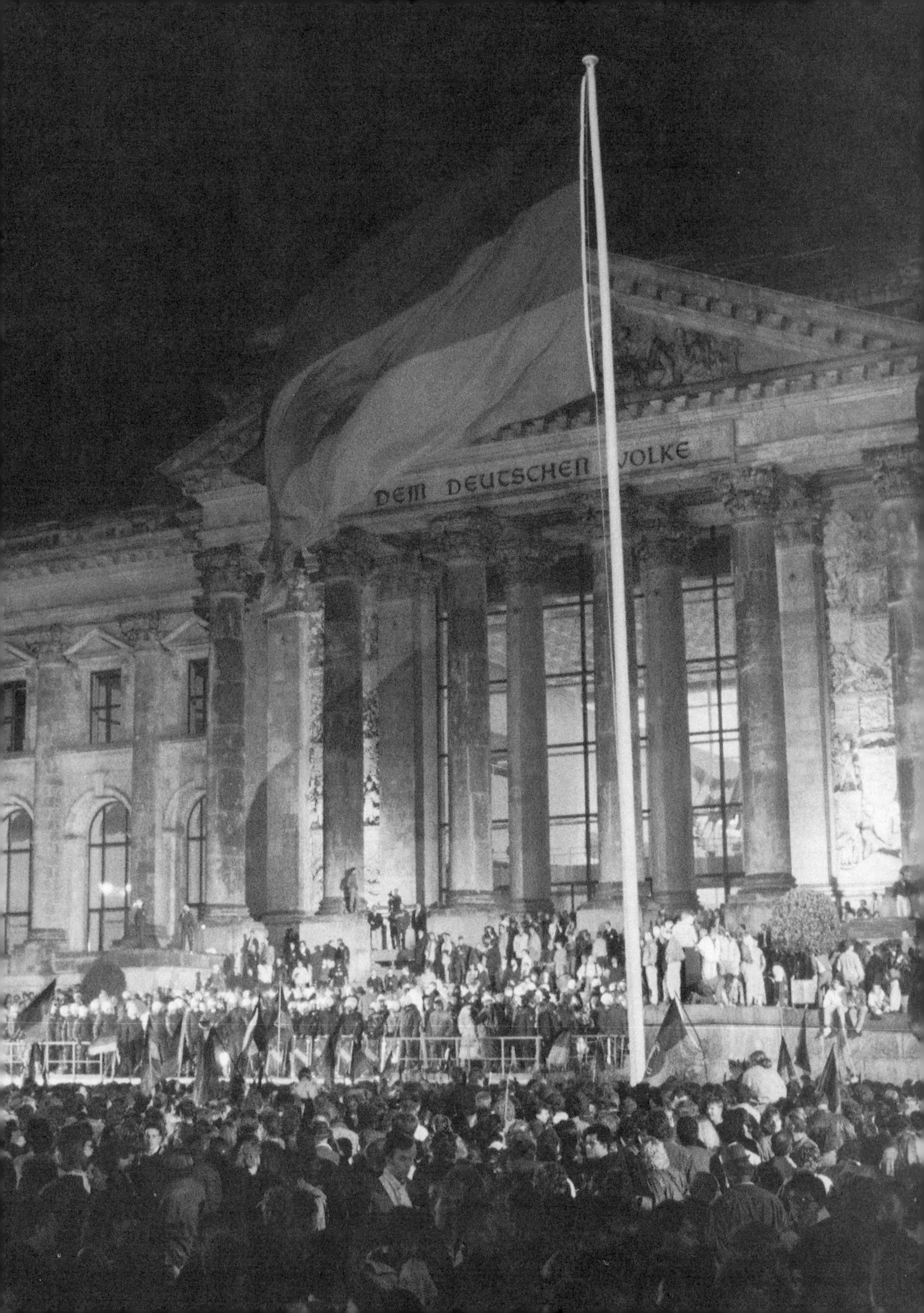
DEM DEUTSCHEN
OLKE

Introduction

SECONDS AFTER MIDNIGHT on October 3, 1990, an enormous black, red, and gold flag rose against the dark sky in Berlin, East Germany.

A breeze caught the flag, fluttering it to life. Suddenly, fireworks lit up the night. Thousands who had gathered in front of the old Reichstag building, the government seat of Germany before 1933, broke into a cheer. Tears flowed and strangers embraced. From the steps of the Reichstag, a choir burst into the words of the national anthem, "Unity and justice and freedom for the German fatherland."

It was a never-to-be-forgotten moment. East and West Germany had reunified, become one country again. They had been separate since the end of World War II, when the former Soviet Union took over the eastern third of Germany and set up a Communist government there.

For over forty years, citizens of the two Germanys had dreamed of ending the separation. Then, almost overnight, the Communists lost control of Eastern Europe. The Berlin Wall fell, borders between East and West Germany reopened, and people were allowed to travel freely back and forth.

Although the two countries were now very different, most Germans were convinced that unification was a desirable next step.

(Opposite page) At midnight, October 3, 1990, a crowd gathers at the Berlin Reichstag, the German house of government, as the new German flag is unfurled to signal the official reunification of Germany.

7

In 1871, Otto von Bismarck became the first chancellor of the German empire after using military force to unite the many independent German states.

Unification is a theme that marches through German history. Around A.D. 800, King Charlemagne united the lands that are now Germany, France, and Italy into a Holy Roman Empire. One thousand years later, a warlike Germany, led by Otto von Bismarck, used "blood and iron [guns]" to again bring parts of France, Italy, as well as Austria under Prussian (German) control.

In the 1900s, Germany dreamed of a larger and more powerful unified homeland or "fatherland." That dream led the country into two disastrous wars. When World War I ended, instead of gaining land, Germany was forced to give up vast amounts of territory to France and Poland.

Defeat in World War II seemed to bring a permanent end to unification hopes. The victorious Allies divided the country into four military zones. Three of those zones were later combined into the Federal Republic of Germany, a democratic nation. The fourth zone became the German Democratic Republic, a country cut off from the free world by concrete walls and wire blockades.

Free elections

Disgraced and divided, East and West Germans never stopped wanting to become one again. Finally, on March 18, 1990, four months after the Wall fell, East Germans were allowed a say in their future. For the first time since World War II, they voted in free elections. Not surprisingly, the majority cast their ballots for a single, reunited Germany.

After October 3, 1990, reunification was a fact. The barbed wire was gone. Germans shared the same borders, the same leaders, the same freedoms.

But in a different sense, reunification was still a work in progress. The excitement, the banners, and the flags had been packed away. The real work began, with both sides finding it hard to work together after so many years. They had

In November 1989, jubilant Berliners topple a section of the Berlin Wall, which had divided their city for almost thirty years. This act symbolized their new freedom and unity.

grown apart. Easterners saw westerners as proud, bossy money-lovers. Westerners perceived the east as lazy, complaining, and unwilling to pay its fair share of reunification costs. Those costs were measured in billions of dollars. Unemployment in the east and taxes in the west seemed to rise every day.

The new Germany had to find answers to tough questions. Could the present government continue to lead its people in spite of growing anger over the cost of reunification? Would money alone solve Germany's problems? Could the world trust a unified Germany to remain peaceful? Would new political hate groups undermine the reunification process?

"Wir sind ein Volk," the people chanted that October night in Dresden, Leipzig, and Berlin: "We are one people." It would take more than dreams and emotion for Germany to become a country with a united vision for the future.

1

East Versus West

IN THE SUMMER of 1945, Germany lay in ruins. In Europe, World War II was over; Hitler and his Nazi government had been destroyed. The great German cities of Berlin, Munich, and Cologne were piles of blackened rubble. Over three million German soldiers had been killed in the fighting. Half a million civilians had died in air raids. German survivors were dazed and bewildered by defeat.

As the fighting ended, four victorious Allies—Britain, France, the Soviet Union, and the United States—decided Germany's future. To avoid chaos and oversee recovery, they temporarily divided the country into four occupation zones, with Soviet troops in the east, British in the northwest, Americans in the southwest, and French in a small zone in the west. Berlin, the country's capital, lay deep within the Soviet zone, but it was also divided into four occupation zones. Each of the Allies established a military government in their zone. No central authority led the defeated country.

The Allies set up four end-of-war objectives. The first was long-term: to reconstruct German political life along democratic lines, readying the country for a peaceful future. (Few suspected that the Soviet Union had other plans.)

(Opposite page) Terrified children huddle outside the ruins of their Nuremberg home during World War II. By the end of the war, Allied bombing had reduced most of Germany's major cities to rubble.

11

Surviving leaders of Germany's Third Reich are tried for war crimes. The Nazi atrocities perpetrated during World War II convinced many people that Germany should never again be allowed to grow strong as a nation.

The second goal, demilitarization, stripped Germany of its weapons. The nation was forbidden to build or develop military equipment that might again lead to war.

Denazification—the removal of Nazi party members and sympathizers from positions of power—was the third objective. This process reached its climax during the Nuremberg Trials of 1945-49, when former Nazis were tried and found guilty of acts of aggression and crimes against humanity.

Over the final objective, the issue of reparations—German payment for suffering and destruction caused by war—the Allies split. Britain, France, and the United States argued that German citizens should not be required to repay their wartime debts until they rebuilt their country and developed a healthy, growing economy. The Soviet Union, however, believed that repayment should begin immediately. In spite of the devastation in Germany, the Soviets began removing goods and equipment from their zone.

Strained relations between the Soviet Union and the Western Allies worsened when Britain, France, and the United States gave their zones more freedom, as well as leading roles in their own economic recovery. The Communist-led Soviet Union refused to loosen its control over the eastern zone. Plans for reunification reached a deadlock that apparently could not be broken.

By 1947, Soviet and Western cooperation had ended. East and west German zones were being reconstructed under entirely different political and economic systems. The United States, Britain, and France unified their three zones early in the year, although joint military occupation continued. Political parties and free elections were established. In June 1948, a new form of money, the deutsche mark (DM), was introduced in all areas except Berlin.

The Soviet Union responded by setting up political parties and a monetary system in their zone. With hopes for a Berlin takeover, they circulated the new money, the Ostmark, throughout all sections of the city. Western leaders countered by introducing the deutsche mark into the capital.

The Berlin airlift

A crisis arose on June 24, 1948. Planning to gain control of the western sections of Berlin, the Soviets blocked all roads, canals, and railroads between the city and the western zone. Electricity was cut off. Two million Berliners in the free zone were left without food, fuel, or supplies.

Winston Churchill, Britain's leader during the war, had already warned the world that an "Iron Curtain" of Communist domination was descending across the continent of Europe. Since the war's end, the Soviet Union had established Communist governments in Bulgaria, Romania, Hungary, and Poland. Churchill recognized the

During the Allied occupation of Germany after World War II, an elderly German woman tries to figure out how much money she now has after exchanging the old, Nazi currency for the new Deutsche marks printed by the Western powers.

An American transport plane approaches the Berlin airport in 1948, bringing supplies to the blockaded city.

Soviets' act in Berlin as one more step in a larger agenda:

> There can be no doubt [that the] Communist Government of Russia has made up its mind to drive us and France and all the other Allies out and turn the Russian zone in Germany into one of its satellite states under the rule of totalitarian terrorism.

Western Allies responded with a massive airlift. Beginning in July, planes loaded with provisions landed in the besieged city at the rate of one every forty-five seconds. The emergency relief continued until May 1949, when the Soviets backed down and lifted the blockade. By then, separate governments had been set up in the city.

Formal acceptance of the country's division soon followed. In May 1949, the unified western zone approved a new federal constitution. On September 21, military occupation ended, and the western zone officially became the Federal Republic of Germany (FRG) with its new capital in Bonn.

That same May, citizens of the eastern zone were presented with a Communist-prepared con-

Grateful Berliners unload bags of coal from an American transport plane during the airlift of 1948.

stitution. On October 7, 1949, the Soviet zone was renamed the German Democratic Republic (GDR), with East Berlin as its capital.

Churchill's vision of the future had been correct. The Federal Republic of Germany and the German Democratic Republic were two countries now, traveling different roads to different futures.

Federal Republic of Germany

With the formation of the Federal Republic of Germany, seventy-three-year-old Konrad Adenauer became chancellor, or head, of the new government. Adenauer, a strong anti-Communist, had been an enemy of the Nazis during the war. Now a leader of the powerful political party the Christian Democratic Union, he was recognized by the Allies and his fellow citizens as an experienced politician who would make sure that West Germany developed under a democratic influence.

The Federal Republic's new constitution established a three-branch government similar to that of the United States. Within the executive branch, a president represented the country at formal and ceremonial functions. However, the chancellor held full leadership power. Members of the two-house legislative branch drew up laws, represented the people, and acted as watchdog over the chancellor and his cabinet. The judicial branch was independent and complex, ready to interpret and uphold the law in the new democratic system.

The constitution, known as the Basic Law, promised every citizen eighteen years of age or older the right to vote by secret ballot in free elections. Freedom of speech, press, worship, and assembly were guaranteed. Political parties (among them the Christian Democratic Union, the Christian Social Union, the Social Democratic party, and the Free Democratic party) were allowed to compete for votes, although extremist

Ludwig Erhard, a staunch capitalist, was West Germany's first minister for economic affairs. Under his leadership, West Germany's economy recovered and quickly prospered.

parties such as the Nazis or Communists were outlawed.

In addition to a central government, ten Länder (similar to states in the United States) were set up, each having its own constitution and government. District and local leaders were elected to deal with such community issues as highways, hospitals, and public utilities.

While Chancellor Adenauer shaped political policy in the Federal Republic, Minister for Economic Affairs Ludwig Erhard set up plans for economic recovery. Erhard believed in a regulated free-market economy similar to those in the United States and Britain. Under his system, citizens and private companies owned and controlled most of West Germany's businesses and services. Consumer demand and competition determined which goods and services were produced and how prices were set. West Germans were free to decide how to earn and spend their money.

With support from the United States and other Allies, the success of Erhard's policies was apparent almost immediately. In 1950, the *New York Times* reported:

> There is striking evidence throughout the republic of the vast improvement in production. This is manifest in large amounts of new construction, the thousands of heavy diesel trucks that clog the super-highways, the well-filled shop windows and the change in the dress and appearance of the middle and upper classes and, to a lesser extent, of the workers.

Leaders of the Federal Republic were convinced that their new country would eventually become stable and successful, a place where citizens could live independent and happy lives.

German Democratic Republic

The constitution of the German Democratic Republic resembled West Germany's constitution, with a representative government, a multi-party system, and guaranteed rights for all. However, from the beginning, the country was under control of the Communist party.

Communism was conceived in 1848 by German philosopher Karl Marx, who was deeply disturbed by the hardships endured by factory and mine workers in France, Britain, and Germany. Marx imagined a system in which there would be no private ownership of land or goods, and everyone would live in peace and prosperity.

Vladimir Lenin, a Russian revolutionary, tried to put Marx's theories into practice in Russia after the overthrow of Czar Nicholas II in 1917. However, in order to ensure the success of Communism there, Lenin, and later Joseph Stalin and other Soviet leaders, ruthlessly put down all opposition. Party members took over leading positions in government, police, military, agriculture, and industry.

The same was true in the newly formed German Democratic Republic. Wilhelm Pieck was

(Left) Karl Marx (1818-1883) provided the intellectual basis for communism with his socialist philosophy. (Right) Vladimir Lenin (1870-1924) put Marx's ideas into practice by establishing a Communist system of government in Russia in 1917.

Soviet leaders named Walter Ulbricht first secretary of the Communist party in East Germany. As such, he was the true ruler of the country.

elected the country's first president, but Soviet leaders established Walter Ulbricht, a devoted German Communist, as first secretary of the Socialist Unity party (Communist party) and highest authority in the new country.

Ulbricht, who had helped found the German Communist Party in 1919, worked closely with the Soviets to lay the groundwork for the new East German government. Under his influence, top governing bodies included an 11-member Council of Ministers, a Council of State, and a 466-member People's Chamber.

In theory, all officials answered to the wishes of the people. A supreme court and district and local courts supposedly guaranteed citizens justice and a voice in selecting these officials. District and local committees supposedly encouraged citizen involvement in political issues.

In practice, however, the East German government operated quite differently. As German historian Louis Snyder pointed out, "Behind the elaborate facade and . . . doublespeak are the denial of basic rights, the exploitation, and the familiar trappings of a police state."

Wilhelm Pieck (right) is welcomed by a member of the East German government upon his election as the first president of the new Communist nation in 1949.

Elections were held regularly, but only Communist-approved candidates could run for office. Participation in local politics was encouraged, but decisions were made at the national level by Communist leaders. Courts were open to all, but judges were Party members of proven loyalty, guaranteed to support Communist policies and beliefs.

The German Democratic Republic's new constitution supported such basic rights as freedom of speech, press, and religion, but citizens did not actually enjoy the same liberty as their neighbors to the west. Newspapers, books, and magazines contained only articles approved by the Communist party. Church membership was discouraged. Informants for the much hated *Stasi* (secret police) were everywhere, with files kept on anyone who spoke out against the system. Critics of the government often found themselves in prison or treated unfairly when it came to jobs or housing opportunities.

State-run economy

East Germany's economy, in contrast to West Germany's, was state-run—centrally planned and managed by the Communist party. Under this system, production levels and prices for agricultural and manufactured goods were set, not by competition or public desire, but by the government. Supply did not always match demand. Goods were distributed, not by need, but according to central economic policy.

Under Ulbricht's leadership, most of East Germany's land, business, industry, transportation, and communication networks were owned and controlled by the government. Individuals might own a small business or piece of land, but the majority was allowed only household goods and personal items such as clothes, books, and radios. Often, these were expensive and difficult to find.

East Germans resented Ulbricht and the Communists who deprived them of their possessions, their land, and their liberty. From the beginning, some had seen the west as a haven of wealth and freedom. As time passed, more and more viewed the Federal Republic as a chance for a better life, a chance too tempting to be ignored.

The Wall

As the Communists continued to oppress East Germans, young professionals and skilled workers fled to West Germany, taking their families and their futures with them. Over 400,000 escaped in 1953. The numbers varied over the next eight years, but never dropped below 170,000 annually. In the summer of 1961, the exodus reached 5,000 people a day.

Two West Berliners help an East German woman escape over the Berlin Wall in 1961. Many people risked—and forfeited— their lives trying to escape from Communist East Berlin into free West Berlin.

(Left) Before the Berlin Wall was built, signs like this, depicting the face of a prisoner in a Soviet zone concentration camp, warned West Berliners of the danger that lay just ahead if they ignored the boundary line between east and west. The sign says "Pay attention—only ten more meters." (Below) Desperate East Berliners squeeze through a tunnel they have dug under the Berlin Wall in 1962. Seventeen family members escaped through the tunnel before it was discovered by East German authorities.

As early as 1952, leaders in the German Democratic Republic began to take steps to stop the flow, first by blocking railway and road traffic both into and out of the country.

Samuel Reber, acting head of the U.S. military force overseeing Germany, quickly recognized the Soviet threat behind the East German action. In a letter to the Soviet commissioner in Berlin dated May 1952, he wrote, "I protest vigorously against these actions, which are manifestly contrary to the interests of the whole German population. . . . I therefore request you to give the necessary instructions to have these measures rescinded."

The Communists refused to cooperate. Instead, leaders in the German Democratic Republic began creating a barbed-wire boundary to stop the

East Berlin children peer across the tangle of barbed wire that separated East Berlin from West Berlin in the summer of 1961. Before the summer had ended, a concrete wall had replaced the barbed wire, effectively sealing off West Berlin.

flow of talent and resources which threatened to destroy the East German economy. Over the years, the 860-mile-long border between East and West Germany became a death strip for anyone trying to cross.

More barriers

Land mines were planted between a double line of ten-foot-high barbed-wire fences. Attack dogs patrolled the most likely escape routes. Trip wires set off alarms and automatic machine guns.

As the barrier cut lines of transportation between the two countries, Berlin, deep inside the German Democratic Republic, became a last avenue of escape. Thousands of easterners poured into West Berlin, where they were welcomed, provided with passports, and allowed to relocate.

Soviet and East German authorities reacted by taking state control of the area. First, they prevented all unauthorized movement between the two sections of the city. Then, in August 1961, they cut off the city's free section from the rest of East Germany.

Chancellor Adenauer had promised to support the city: "Whatever may happen, Berlin can be sure that it will be aided by the Federal Republic with all the means within its power." However, he hesitated to act for fear of provoking a war with the Soviet Union. The United States also hesitated, although Vice President Lyndon Johnson stated while visiting the country that summer that "this arbitrary splitting of the city of Berlin is a flagrant violation of solemn international agreements and obligations undertaken by the Soviet Government."

Soon it was too late. The Berlin Wall—forty-five miles of reinforced concrete slicing the city in two—was quickly completed. Only a narrow highway remained to connect West Berlin with the Federal Republic.

Armed guards watch as workmen set in place a huge concrete slab during the erection of the Berlin Wall in 1961.

Suddenly, teachers, mechanics, physicians, and businesspeople who lived in East Berlin and traveled to work in West Berlin could no longer reach their jobs. Easterners were permanently separated from friends and relatives in the west.

Escapes

Stubbornly, East Germans refused to give up their quest for freedom. One family rigged up a hot air balloon and drifted across the border. Oth-

West Berlin police officers lend a hand as an East Berlin woman is aided in her escape from the Communist side.

ers swam rivers, dodging hails of Communist bullets, to reach the west.

In Berlin, some easterners began jumping across the border from open windows in buildings above the Wall. They leaped into fire nets, or took their chances as they hit the pavement. When authorities responded by bricking up the windows, people tunneled under the Wall. The most desperate scrambled over despite armed border guards who shot to kill. One highly publicized incident involved eighteen-year-old Peter Fechter, a bricklayer, who was cut down by machine gun fire as he tried to scale the Wall. He died alone in its shadow.

Hatred of the Wall grew with the passing years. Berliners dubbed it *Schandmauer*, or Wall of Shame. In the west, its cement slabs became a canvas for graffiti artists who let out their anger with slogans such as "Smash the Wall" and "Walls are not everlasting." In places, white crosses marked East German escape attempts that had failed.

More than just a barrier, the Wall became a symbol of the Communist system that divided East and West Germany. As the two countries went their separate ways, reunification, buried under tons of barbed wire and concrete, seemed like a dream destined never to come true.

2

Freedom!

IN THE YEARS following the rise of the Berlin Wall, the existence of two Germanys became an accepted, although regrettable, fact of life. West Germany joined several international organizations, including the European Economic Community (EEC) and the North Atlantic Treaty Organization (NATO). East Germany became a member of the Warsaw Pact, an Eastern European military alliance under Soviet command, and eventually established diplomatic ties with more than 120 nations including France, Great Britain, and the United States.

In the early summer of 1973, the Federal Republic of Germany (FRG) signed a goodwill treaty with the German Democratic Republic (GDR), formally recognizing the republic as a second German state. The pact, brought about through the efforts of West German chancellor Willy Brandt, called for the development of good neighbor relations, the observance of human rights, the upholding of frontiers, and the renunciation of force.

Friendlier feelings now existed between the two countries; mutual suspicion was reduced. Even the Communists, always critical of the West, expressed relief. "The curtain has opened completely. The clouds that seemed to darken the

(Opposite page) In November 1989, with East Berlin's Communist regime officially over, thousands of West Berliners scramble atop the Berlin Wall to peer into East Berlin.

future have disappeared," East German leader Erich Honecker affirmed.

The good life

By the 1980s, leaders in the Federal Republic of Germany could boast that their citizens lived in one of the most well-to-do and progressive countries in the Western world. More than two million people were "Deutsche-mark millionaires" (worth over $500,000). Middle-class West Germans worked on average 37.5 hours per week, as compared to the U.S. forty-hour work week. They owned gracious homes, drove well-made cars, and shopped in stores bulging with material goods. All workers, even recent high school graduates, received six weeks' paid vacation from work every year. Health care and welfare benefits were almost universal and regarded as inalienable rights.

On the other side of the Wall, East German leaders, also proudly, claimed that their country had the highest standard of living in the Communist world. In comparison to horse-drawn farm equipment used in Poland, East Germany used modern tractors and combine harvesters on its collectivized farms. (These farms consisted of large tracts of land owned by the government and worked by the people for a wage.) In industry, there had been developments in microelectronics and computers, as well as continued growth in such traditional areas as chemical and optical technology.

With guaranteed employment, almost every East German had a job, plus such benefits as free health care, unemployment insurance, and retirement pensions. Although luxuries such as televisions, refrigerators, and automobiles were scarce, many could afford them. "Certainly it is no kingdom of heaven," one East German sociology pro-

No match for the West German-made Mercedes-Benz or BMW, these East German-made Trabants sit unsold in a field in Czechoslovakia. Once East Germans could buy western products, they ignored the inferior merchandise available from the Communist bloc.

fessor admitted, "but a lot has been achieved."

In spite of the German Democratic Republic's claims to success, however, the country's wealth could not compare with that of the west. Everyday life in the east was gray and somber. Homes and apartments were often cramped and crumbling. Those automobiles that were available were tinny, unreliable Wartburgs and Trabants that could not compare to the west's gleaming Mercedes and BMWs. Necessities such as bread and potatoes might be cheap, but specialty items, including fruit and some vegetables, were rare and expensive. East Germans grumbled that their choices were often between cabbages and more cabbages.

Limited luxuries

The Kaisers were one example of an average East German family. Joachim, Gitta, and their daughter Janine lived in a small five-room apartment in Potsdam, on the outskirts of Berlin. Their rent was low, only 47.50 Ostmarks (about $27.00) a month. Yet the television set that Joachim proudly displayed in the living room had cost almost half a year's wages.

Every day, on that television, the Kaisers

watched advertisements for western luxuries denied them in their own country. As a wide variety of personal care products available in the west danced across the screen, Gitta and Janine thought of the single brand of inferior hand soap available to them and the foul-smelling, sticky hair spray sold in government-owned beauty shops. Joachim, seeing the beautiful cars advertised for sale in the west, wondered unhappily if he would ever see the new Trabant he had ordered fourteen years before. If it came, it would cost the Kaisers around thirty thousand marks, or approximately two-and-a-half years' pay.

Voices for change

While East Germans grew more discontented with their circumstances, life for citizens in many other Communist countries was even worse. Working-class Romanians suffered persecution and poverty while the corrupt ruling class lived in luxury. Polish citizens struggled to survive under a centralized economy that was in shambles. Even the powerful Soviet Union, long time overseer of Eastern Europe, faced an economic crisis that forced its people to stand in bread lines and threatened the country's continued existence.

As economic problems grew in the Communist bloc, so did movements for freedom and a better way of life. In Poland, the Solidarity party (an organization of trade unions) boldly led protest demonstrations that demanded better living conditions and economic and political reforms. Soviet leader Mikhail Gorbachev, foreseeing approaching economic disaster for his country, announced his new policy of *perestroika*—political and economic restructuring—that would move the Soviet Union closer to the market democracies of the West.

Gorbachev continued to pave the way for fur-

In the late 1980s, Soviet leader Mikhail Gorbachev, fearing the economic collapse of the Soviet Union and its satellites, initiated sweeping economic reforms.

ther reform when he made known his "unqualified recognition of the integrity and security of every state and its right to choose freely its own political and social system as well as unqualified adherence to the norms and principles of international law, especially respect for the right of peoples to self-determination."

The Soviet leader also urged Polish Communists to support that country's newly elected prime minister, Tadeusz Mazowiecki, a member of Solidarity and a non-Communist. The action signaled the end of four decades of totalitarian rule in Poland. As Mazowiecki took office in September 1989, he announced that his government would move ahead to establish democracy and create a market economy.

Encouraged, East Germany began demanding change as well. At first, discontent was voiced only behind the doors of churches, the sole institutions in the country not controlled by the Communist government. Since 1978, the Communists had allowed more religious freedom than in earlier times. But the demands for reform outgrew the church and blossomed into public demonstrations. Soon public outcry could no longer be ignored by Erich Honecker, aging leader of the German Democratic Republic.

Polish prime minister Tadeusz Mazowiecki casts his vote in Poland's 1990 presidential election, the first Polish popular election. Poland's fight for civil liberties inspired many East Germans to demand more freedoms, too.

Hard-line Communist

Honecker had come to power when he succeeded Walter Ulbricht as head of the Communist party in 1971. Born in 1912, he joined the Party in 1929, had been imprisoned by the Nazis during World War II, and later studied Communist theory in the Soviet Union.

Always a hard-line Communist, Honecker was highly critical of the liberalization taking place in the Soviet Union. His response to his country's demands was to set in motion more repressive re-

East German leader Erich Honecker and his wife, Margot, leave the hospital where he was recovering from surgery. Honecker, a hard-line Communist, was deposed and later arrested.

forms—calling out the dreaded State Security police, forcing dissenters into hiding, and renewing his "shoot to kill" orders for anyone caught trying to escape from East Germany.

Hole in the Iron Curtain

Pressure for change in Eastern Europe was strong. By the late summer of 1989, Honecker's days in power were numbered.

Hungary, one of the more progressive of the Communist bloc countries, made the next move. Encouraged by Gorbachev's words, Hungary's Communist party promised unrestricted elections and better opportunities for private ownership of land and business. In a daring move, it ordered the barbed wire torn down that ran along Hungary's border with free Austria.

In November 1989, more than a million East Germans turned out in East Berlin for a demonstration calling for political reforms in their country.

East Germans traveling in Hungary were quick to take advantage of this new chance for escape. Hundreds fled, leaving cars and luggage behind. The Hungarian government did nothing to stop them. What began as a trickle of families soon became a flood. In just one four-day span in mid-September 1989, more than thirteen thousand East Germans escaped to Austria and then on to West Germany.

A warm welcome awaited them there. They were immediately granted West German citizenship with all its rights and privileges. Camps were set up until permanent homes could be found.

Behind the Wall, East Germans could not ignore these momentous events. Increasing numbers of demonstrators took to the streets, demanding reform at home. Others decided that the time was right to make a break for freedom. Fleeing

In August 1989, taking advantage of a new, relaxed security between Communist Hungary and free Austria, these East Germans escape into Austria. In the weeks that followed, thousands of East Germans would do likewise.

south through Czechoslovakia and Hungary, escapees crossed the open borders there. Some took refuge in West German embassies in Czechoslovakia and Poland. There they obtained transportation to the west.

Threat to stability

This exodus soon posed a threat to the stability of both Germanys. The FRG had to somehow absorb tens of thousands of refugees needing jobs and housing. East German leaders grappled with a more serious problem. The mass escapes were an embarrassing replay of the years before the Wall. They implied the failure of the Communist system and threatened the future of East Germany itself. If escapes continued, there soon would be too few productive citizens left for the country to function.

East Germans line up for breakfast in a Hungarian refugee camp in 1989. Many left everything behind in East Germany in order to gain their freedom.

A tearful East German mother bids farewell to her daughter who, with other refugees, has sought asylum at the West German embassy in Prague, Czechoslovakia, in 1989.

But no one, especially Erich Honecker, suffering from cancer, seemed willing to take the drastic step of closing the borders around the entire country to stop the departures. While his government denounced Hungary for "engaging in the organized smuggling of humans," Honecker concentrated on his plans for East Germany's celebration of forty years under Communist rule.

Promises of reform

That left other more practical members of the East German Communist party to confront and deal with the enormous unrest. Encouraged by Gorbachev, who attended the fortieth anniversary celebration, they reluctantly began to take steps toward change.

On October 18, 1989, they replaced Honecker with Egon Krenz, another Communist, but one who promised to begin reforming the govern-

(Below) Liberal Communist Egon Krenz clasps his hands victoriously after winning the election as East Germany's new leader in October 1989. Krenz promised to reform the government.

ment. One of Krenz's first pronouncements was to set forth limited travel concessions—citizens would be permitted to travel outside East German borders for four weeks a year.

To people hungry for real reform, this was not enough. The stream of refugees continued unabated. It included carpenters, bakers, schoolteachers, engineers, cooks, dentists, and steelworkers. Doctors left in especially large numbers, probably because they earned less than $3,500 a month in the east. In the west, they could earn three times that much.

Demonstrations in large East German cities like Dresden and Leipzig grew in size and number. "In one day, [we] can be out of here," crowds chanted threateningly.

The Wall comes down

When they realized that the Iron Curtain was full of holes, East German officials decided that they could make only one choice. Political researcher Ronald Asmus noted, "If they used repressive force now, that would only fuel the exodus."

Bowing to public pressure, the entire Council of Ministers—the official government of East Germany—resigned on November 7, 1989. On November 9, a Communist spokesperson announced that the Berlin Wall no longer served any purpose and that all travel restrictions were lifted. The East German people were at liberty to come and go as they pleased.

The announcement electrified both of the Germanys and the world. While bewildered East German guards looked on, East and West Berliners rushed to the Wall. Some climbed over it. Others danced on it. Celebrants hacked and hammered at the concrete, knocking loose large chunks.

The scene was like Thanksgiving, Christmas,

Thousands of East Berliners and West Berliners meet at a breach in the Berlin Wall in November 1989 after restrictions were lifted.

and New Year's Eve rolled into one. Long-separated loved ones met, laughed, and cried. Champagne corks popped. At 3 A.M. the streets were still filled with the noise of honking horns and happy shouts. Some of the newly liberated carried suitcases. Others only wanted to satisfy their curiosity, to walk the few steps through the barricade to the glittering Kurfürstendamm, West Berlin's fashionable shopping boulevard. After a few hours of window-shopping, they returned to their homes, momentarily satisfied.

"There is so much color, so much light," Karin Tittman, an East Berliner, marveled.

A new direction

As the ecstatic public tried to assimilate the changes that had occurred in their countries, both

German governments set to work putting together plans that would chart the direction of East Germany in the days to come.

East German leaders were first with their proposal. On November 10, one day after the Wall fell, the Communist party set forth a platform that included free elections and a planned market economy. While the country would retain its socialist character, the Party would step back from its position of control in the government.

West Germans, led by Chancellor Helmut Kohl, countered with an alternative proposal—a ten-point plan that called for slow improvement of relations between East and West Germany. East Germans would have a voice in the direction of the country through democratic elections. Eventually, the two countries would become one.

Berliners from east and west sit and dance on the Berlin Wall to celebrate the beginning of a new year, a new decade, and a new era in their country's history.

Kohl's plan was immediately rejected by Communist leaders who insisted that the GDR remain a separate country.

Debate over reunification

Once again, the public made its feelings known. East German anger at the Communists led to further resignations in the government. With the Communist dominance broken, delegates from twelve anti-Communist political groups stepped in to help determine the country's future. The majority called for a new constitution and recommended that elections take place by May 6, 1990. They also approved Kohl's plan, including its goal of eventual reunification.

Weidervereinigung! Reunification! The word was on everyone's lips and controversy abounded. Many believed that reunification was the logical next step in German history, a process that would lead to greatness and wealth. Others argued that reunification was an impractical notion held by old men living in the past. If attempted, it could spell ruin for West Germany.

Time was needed to find solutions to such debate, but time was limited. The reunification process, once set in motion, rushed onward, guided by Germany's leaders, but fueled by the will of the people themselves.

West German chancellor Helmut Kohl countered the East German Communist leaders' proposal for reforms with a ten-point plant that included reunification.

3

Unification: Dream or Nightmare?

THE OPENING OF the Wall entwined the lives and spirits of Germans as never before. Whatever differences existed, whatever the future held, all agreed that the main task of the days ahead would be mapping out a new system of government based on something other than Communist repression.

"What lies behind us is a system . . . based on fear," pointed out Markus Meckel, an East German Social Democrat. "What we are seeking is justice for all."

But what did that justice call for? East Germans had suffered under an oppressive rule for forty years. Their country was in desperate circumstances. The economy was shaky, the government on the defensive, the days ahead uncertain. Did not justice demand that easterners have a chance to achieve the wealth and freedom enjoyed by the west?

West Germans, on the other hand, had humbled themselves after the war, learned the lessons of democracy, and rebuilt their country from rubble.

(Opposite page) The price of freedom: East German factory workers protest the closing of their plant in the fall of 1992. The placard reads "German unification, freedom, unemployment!?"

They had worked hard to achieve the wealth they now enjoyed. While all wanted their eastern brothers and sisters to enjoy equal good fortune, they asked themselves whether justice required them to assume responsibility for the east's problems.

The next step

Many Germans, Chancellor Helmut Kohl and his Christian Democratic Union included, argued that reunification would permanently heal the painful wound of separation that both countries had endured since the end of World War II. Union with the wealthy west was also the quickest route to a rosy future for the struggling East Germans.

The process would not be easy; Kohl himself expressed caution. "We cannot give guarantees. . . . We must roll up our shirt sleeves and help each other." Nevertheless, the unification of the two countries would provide money and leadership necessary to correct the enormous problems caused by years of communism.

Other Germans were not convinced that a single Germany would be best for all. Forty years had created too many differences for the two countries to become one again. Enormous compromises would be necessary. In the end, would anyone be happy?

Seventeen-year-old Eve Droschler believed that she would not be happy with a single Germany. Eve was a gifted East German student who had enjoyed a free education under the old system. "I don't want to live in a capitalist system like the U.S.A. There is nothing I really want to buy," she said, perhaps worried that shopping malls and fast food restaurants would be a poor exchange for her secure life in East Germany thus far.

Diplomats, politicians, scholars, and journalists

around the world debated the question for months. The French, remembering World War II, feared that a larger and more powerful Germany might again become an enemy. Polish leaders worried that unresolved border disputes between their country and Germany might resurface when the east became independent of the Soviet Union. The Soviets expressed concern that a unified Germany would side with the West against them, leaving them to solve their own economic troubles unaided.

In the end, however, the East German public again had the final word. Elections, at first set for May 1990, were pushed forward to March. Citizens who had not been allowed to participate in

East Germans line up early on election day, eager, after forty years of repression, to exercise their right to vote. A record 93 percent turned out.

free elections since November 1932 went to the polls in a record 93 percent turnout. (Only an estimated 54 percent of eligible voters turned out for the 1992 U.S. presidential election.) East Germans handed a resounding victory to the conservative coalition, a group led by the Christian Democratic Union, who supported early reunification.

For better or worse, East Germans had firmly set their feet on the fast track to reunification. They were convinced that their fondest dreams—freedom and a higher standard of living—could be best and most quickly satisfied through a merger with the prosperous Federal German Republic. They were willing to make any sacrifice to translate those dreams into reality.

Costs involved

East Germans wanted reunification and all the benefits it would provide. West Germans were willing, provided the price they paid was not too great.

Even by optimistic estimates, that price would not be small. East German factories and equipment were outdated and needed to be brought up to modern standards. Roads had not been repaired since the Communists came to power. Communication networks were primitive; only 17 percent of East German households had telephones. Cleanup of environmental pollution alone would require hundreds of millions of deutsche marks.

The West German government estimated that total cost of unification per year would be about 40 billion deutsche marks (DM 40 billion) or more than 22 billion dollars. Those costs would continue for at least ten years.

Where would the money come from? The chancellor assured his already highly taxed citizens that no new taxes would be necessary. Pri-

Crumbling East German tenements symbolize the crumbling economy of the east, which would take a big injection of West German capital to rebuild.

vate investment and government backed "unity bonds" (interest-bearing certificates issued by the government) could provide part of the total. Income from surviving East German industry would supply another portion. If all else failed, the government was resolved to borrow the money and temporarily let the federal budget deficit grow.

The government's unification plan was as wide-ranging as its title implied—*Treaty Between the Federal Republic of Germany and the German Democratic Republic Establishing a Monetary, Economic and Social Union.* Experts called it the GEMSU Treaty for short. The plan included reforms—monetary, economic, and environmental among others—that would go far to combine the two countries into one. As a whole, it appeared to provide a complete and practical frame-

This antiquated railway system reflects the outmoded and inadequate infrastructure of East Germany. Roads, transportation, and communications were in desperate need of renewal.

work for union.

The first critical step toward unification was set to take place beginning July 1, 1990. At that time, both East and West Germany would begin to share a single official currency, the deutsche mark. Leaders of both Germanys hoped that by quickly replacing the almost worthless Ostmark, East Germans could improve their economic status while remaining in the east. (The flow of refugees into West Germany continued, although the promise of unification had already slowed the movement from around twenty-three hundred to less than twelve hundred per week.) The benevolent terms of the treaty allowed ordinary citizens to convert most of their money at a one-to-one rate; that is, for every Ostmark they turned in, they received one deutsche mark in return. The GEMSU Treaty emphasized competition and prices based on supply and demand, making united Germany economically comparable to the FGR and other Western countries. The treaty also declared private ownership to be one of the central pillars of the new Germany and abolished large state-owned businesses.

Treuhand

To dispose of those businesses, a government organization, the Trust Fund Institution (*Treuhandanstalt*, or *Treuhand* for short), was formed, headed by former steel industry leader, Detlev Rohwedder. Treuhand employees numbered over three thousand; most worked in eastern Berlin's old Luftwaffe building, once headquarters of the Nazi air force.

The first task of the Treuhand was to evaluate the approximately eight thousand state-owned enterprises left over from the Communist era with the goal of transferring them into the hands of private businesspeople, if possible. The organiza-

A German cyclist rides along holding the oversized likeness of a one-mark coin announcing the "German currency union." The West German Deutsche mark replaced the worthless East German Ostmark in 1990.

tion was given authority to subdivide those businesses, decide if their smaller units could make a profit in the new competitive economy, and sell them or close them down as the case demanded. The Treuhand also had the authority to make loans and approve credit for new buyers.

Environmental reform

Environmental reform was also a critical part of the treaty. Due to ignorance and abuse, the East German environment had been tremendously damaged during forty years of Communist rule. GDR officials admitted that their country's use of brown coal as a primary energy source made them the highest per capita producer of sulfur dioxide in the world. Some 5.2 million tons of the poison spewed into the sky every year.

An East German chemical factory near Leipzig spews pollution right out on the street. Reunification entailed a mammoth environmental cleanup of the east, which had had no pollution controls.

In Bitterfield, near Leipzig, heart of the chemical industry, the sky was always brown, and the heavily polluted air caused respiratory illnesses in most children. Untreated waste poured into the nearby river. Families reluctantly picnicked on the shores of Silver Lake, so named for the many chemicals that shimmered in its waters. The incidence of cancer was high.

Bitterfield was not alone in its dilemma. Some fifteen thousand toxic waste dumps leached contaminants into soil and groundwater across the east. A third of the nation's rivers were contaminated. Air pollution in many large cities was ten to one hundred times higher than safe levels.

The GEMSU Treaty called for an Environmental Union to set up and monitor cleanup programs. New equipment for business and industry had to satisfy the same responsible environmental standards that applied in the Federal Republic.

Existing equipment in the east was required to be brought up to standards within five years.

Social and fiscal reform

The GEMSU Treaty also reformed social and fiscal systems (affairs relating to taxes and the public treasury) in East Germany to bring them into line with those operating in the west. Five Länder (states) and their governments that had been abolished by the Communists after World War II were re-established—Brandenburg, Mecklenburg-Western Pomerania, Saxony, Saxony-Anhalt and Thuringia.

Corporation taxes were initiated. An income tax was set up. While both countries already provided their citizens with generous unemployment, health, pension, and accident benefits, under the new government East Germans were required to contribute a portion of their salary toward those benefits, rather than enjoying them without charge as they had in the past.

Controversy

The GEMSU Treaty got the reunification process underway at top speed. Although the countries were scheduled to remain formally separate until October 3, monetary and economic union took place on July 1 as planned.

At first no one fully grasped the complications surrounding the impending merger. Still, everyone was hopeful that with strong leadership and a little patience, the transition would be smooth. Almost immediately, however, debate, controversy, and a heavy dose of reality complicated the proceedings.

The Treuhand came under criticism for its slowness in restructuring and selling East German businesses. At the sluggish rate at which for-

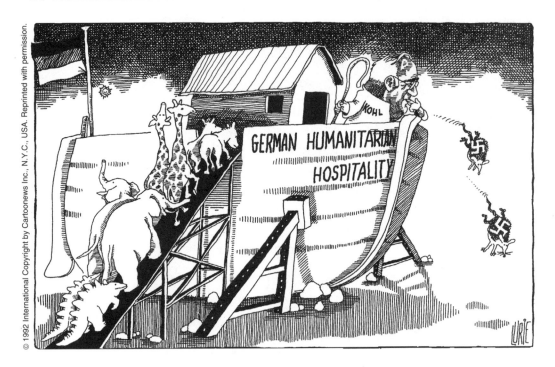

mer state-owned companies were being transferred into private hands, the eastern economy would collapse long before significant change could be achieved.

Eastern-based groups such as the Alliance 90, a coalition made up of the activist New Forum and Democracy Now parties, complained of being left out of discussions about their country's future. They had been bold enough to risk their freedom, even their lives, to fight against the Communist regime before 1989. Now they believed that they were being relegated to the status of observers.

Overcoming obstacles

Scandal reared its ugly head when East German prime minister Lothar de Maiziere and other government officials were accused of acting as informers for East Germany's *Stasi*, the infamous secret police. De Maiziere, a soft-spoken lawyer who had trained as a viola player in his youth, denied the charges.

None of these problems posed any serious threat to unification, but complications from outside the country did. The four World War II Allies—Britain, France, the United States, and the Soviet Union—were still technically responsible for Germany, principally to ensure that it never again became an aggressor nation. The Allies' consent was necessary before unification plans could continue. If they decided that a larger, more powerful Germany might jeopardize world peace, they could oppose unification and block the process.

Most concerns were overcome when Germany agreed never to manufacture or possess nuclear, biological, and chemical weapons, never to reclaim land lost to Poland, and to continue to work closely within the European Community.

Soviet objections remained, however. East Germany's membership in the Warsaw Pact was necessary to provide counterbalance to the powerful North Atlantic Treaty Organization (NATO), a military alliance between Western

East German prime minister Lothar de Maiziere was accused of having been an informant for the secret police during the pre-reform years. Some Germans saw this as scandalous and a possible hindrance to reunification.

countries. If East Germany's reunion with the west resulted in the transfer of its loyalty to NATO, the balance of power would be disturbed.

West German foreign minister Hans-Dietrich Genscher hastened to state that his country wanted to have "very close relations with the Soviet Union" in spite of changing boundaries. Any lingering Soviet objections were overcome as the Communist bloc broke apart, and the Soviets themselves established closer ties to the West.

"Two-Plus-Four"

Representatives of the four former Allies and the two Germanys met in mid-September 1990, at a conference known as the "Two-Plus-Four." There the Allies surrendered their remaining rights as occupying powers in Germany as they signed the *Treaty on the Final Settlement with*

On September 12, 1990, representatives (seated, left to right) from the United States, Great Britain, the Soviet Union, France, and the two Germanys signed the Treaty on the Final Settlement with Respect to Germany.

Respect to Germany. The act gave the go-ahead for the two countries to unite.

The fall of the Berlin Wall had been a triumphant moment in the history of Germany. Eleven months later, on October 3, 1990, an equally memorable celebration took place. Two countries were united as one. Over seventy-seven million people came together after more than forty years of separation.

The price of unification had been calculated. Terms had been set. Treaties had been signed. Germans were aware that costs other than monetary had to be reckoned with and that old wounds would take time to heal. Nevertheless, their hearts swelled as the freedom bells rang out, and the flag of a unified country sailed proudly overhead.

In the words of Soviet foreign minister Eduard Shevardnadze: "[The two Germanys] have closed the book on World War II and started a new age."

4

The Price of Unity

ALTHOUGH FORECASTS FOR a unified Germany seemed bright, many Germans were already doubtful about what the new age would hold for them. In a relatively short time, Helmut Kohl's predicted annual price tag of DM 40 billion ($22.4 billion) had begun to look as out of date as East German industry.

In a blunder that many called scandalous, the government had neglected to take into account a number of reunification costs. The national debt from the former country of East Germany stood at DM 26 billion. Added to that was DM 7 billion promised by the west to help shore up the failing eastern school system plus DM 12 billion committed to help the struggling Soviets remove their troops from German soil. No one dared calculate the additional sums needed to bring vast numbers of nearly bankrupt eastern cities back to life.

By October 1990, revised costs for the coming year had climbed to DM 140 billion (over $95 billion). In 1991, outlay for ten years was predicted to reach DM 1.5 trillion ($1 trillion).

"We have to admit that we miscalculated," confessed economics minister Jürgen Möllemann.

Hard times for eastern Germany

No one had quite grasped how crippled the East German economy had become. Few had

(Opposite page) Abandoned buildings and outdated transportation were the norm in East Germany under the Communist regime. Officials preparing for reunification severely underestimated the amount of capital needed to restore the east's dilapidated infrastructure.

Because of outmoded production facilities, many East German factories would be closed down after reunification. These workers and thousands of others feared that reunification would only mean losing their jobs.

foreseen that eastern Germans might have to wait years, perhaps decades, before they achieved the high standard of living that the west enjoyed.

Now the unpleasant truth was known. The Communists had concealed the true state of the east's economy. Business and industry had failed to modernize because funds had been directed elsewhere by the government. Operating techniques were outmoded. Production of manufactured goods had dropped 50 percent in the nine years prior to 1989. Exports were down as well.

"Their scientific and technological structure is disastrous," said one east-west specialist from the Institute for International Politics in West Berlin.

Unemployment

The mammoth costs of renovating the east stunned Germany and the world, but the figure was insignificant compared to the skyrocketing amounts that would be needed to support and re-train the unemployed. No one had anticipated that the Treuhand would close thousands of all eastern German businesses by mid-1992, throwing enormous numbers of people out of work.

Adding to the problem was the Communist policy of guaranteed jobs, a practice that had swelled employment figures at each facility. In one automobile plant in Zwickau, ninety-three hundred workers built two hundred Trabants in a two-shift day. In the United States, auto companies would have hired fewer than two thousand workers to produce three times as many cars in the same amount of time.

Each plant closure pushed high numbers of eastern German workers into unemployment lines. By the end of 1991, official unemployment fig-

ures in eastern Germany topped 14 percent. Another 20 percent of the eastern work force marked time in government-supported retraining programs, bringing jobless totals to over three million.

Hard work, low wages

The picture was almost as dismal for those who did have work. Leonhard "Hardy" Hanson was one of those lucky ones. Hardy was an electrician who started his own business in 1990, working out of his home.

Making a living in the east was not easy, as Hardy could testify. Not only did he fight against the depressed economy and a shortage of funds to invest in his business, he was handicapped by the east's inadequate phone system. Along with thou-

East German schoolchildren gaze longingly at a store window full of newly available, western-made school supplies. Unfortunately, the high unemployment rate following reunification made purchasing such things difficult.

sands of others, the Hanson family had no telephone. Hardy had no choice but to share a single phone booth with two hundred other people in his neighborhood. Prospective customers either came to his home or sent him a postcard if they wanted his services. Not surprisingly, business was slow.

Everyone in the east paid dearly for reunification, if not with their jobs, then with high prices, low wages, and deteriorating living conditions.

The cost of living was on the rise in the east. Expensive western merchandise had replaced cheaper Communist-era goods on store shelves. The government no longer supported artificially low prices; landlords, entrepreneurs, indeed, anyone who wanted to survive, boosted rates in order to make a profit. "My parents' rent was raised ten times last month," one easterner complained.

At the same time, wages remained low. Hardy and his wife's combined annual income of slightly more than DM 36,000 ($22,000) was roughly a third of what they could have made working in western Germany. "Now that we can buy everything," Edeltraud Hanson, Hardy's wife, observed, "we don't have enough money."

Reunification had been promoted as salvation for the east. Instead it seemed to be just the opposite. Without government funds once provided by the Communists, many hospitals, libraries, and day-care centers were forced to close. For a time, garbage collection was discontinued. Streets were not lighted at night.

Easterners head west

Discouraged by worsening conditions, many easterners chose not to continue the struggle. Between 1989 and mid-1992, over 250,000 easterners moved west. Their actions pushed the situation from bad to worse. With no truck drivers to make deliveries, food and other necessities sim-

The owner of a neighborhood grocery in the eastern German town of Satzkorn chats with a regular customer. The intimacy of such small stores is fast disappearing as western supermarket chains move into eastern Germany.

ply gathered dust in warehouses. Struggling businesses shut down because they could not get the goods needed to keep operating. "Help Wanted" signs replaced displays in store windows. Those who remained in the east asked themselves how recovery could take place if industry was deprived of the talent and resources it so desperately needed.

A handful of easterners, like Kurt Biedenkopf, prime minister of Saxony, was optimistic. "As things pick up here, they will come back and bring with them exactly the kind of expertise we lack," he explained.

Biedenkopf's outlook addressed only the long term. Present conditions were undeniably bleak. If the situation was to improve, if people were to remain and rebuild, help from outside the region was essential.

Easterners' hopes were focused on the west, where reunification did not strike to the heart of life. Even in the west, however, reunification costs had a powerful impact on an economy that had been one of the most stable and healthy in the world.

Western sacrifice

At the end of the 1980s, West Germany had been well known and respected for its solid prosperity. Inflation, one measure of economic well-being, was at a comfortable low, just above 3 percent. The federal budget deficit was manageable. The country ranked second in the world in foreign trade. Only the United States, the Soviet Union, and Japan topped its overall production of manufactured goods.

With the beginning of reunification, however, some of that stability was shaken. The continual transfer of billions of Deutsche marks to the east began to strain the federal budget. So did the demands of thousands of easterners who were moving west and required welfare and unemployment support. Confronted with growing expenses, the government realized that unity bonds and private investment were not bringing in adequate money to support the reunification project.

Finance Minister Theo Waigel took steps nec-

Kurt Biedenkopf, prime minister of the eastern German state of Saxony, was optimistic that the east's economy would slowly but surely recover.

German minister of finance Theo Waigel struggled to discover ways to increase revenues without hurting the economy further.

essary to address this shortage of funds. Immediately after the general election in December 1990, he imposed a temporary 7.5 percent tax on top of the existing income tax. In addition, he taxed insurance premiums, gasoline, and cigarettes. When that new income failed to meet reunification needs, he allowed the federal budget deficit to grow and initiated changes in areas he hoped would least aggravate the public. The defense budget was cut. A number of free health-care provisions were eliminated. Plans were made to sell the debt-ridden, government-run railways.

Westerners rebel

Western Germans, some of the best-paid workers in the world (receiving an average of $23 an hour in wages and benefits compared to $15 for Americans and $16 for Japanese), were also among the most highly taxed. The government's broken promises and higher taxes outraged them. "The state is taking money out of our pockets," claimed magazine editor Rolf Schmidt-Holtz. "The people are embittered because they are being deceived. . . . Billions are trickling away in the east to no effect."

In the spring of 1992, belligerent government employees went to the bargaining table, demanding a raise to compensate for reunification expenses they had been forced to pay. Their demands went unanswered. The government could not afford to pay higher wages. An increase would fuel inflation and increase the growing gap between governmental income and expenditure.

"The simple fact is that we cannot live beyond our means in the long term," Chancellor Kohl cautioned.

Workers disregarded the warning. In May, protesting the government's lack of response, garbage collectors and mail carriers in the west

went on strike. For two weeks, piles of garbage lined the streets and stacks of mail went undelivered as public employees stayed off their jobs.

Forced to decide whether or not they would add a long, paralyzing strike to the country's problems, government representatives relented and granted the pay raises.

For better or worse, that crisis passed. But western Germans began to face the fact that their days of sacrifice had returned. Their comfortable lives were undergoing a disagreeable change. As much as they might grumble and complain, there was nothing to do but make the best of it.

Bags of trash accumulate on this Berlin street in 1992 while government-employed garbage collectors are out on strike to protest heavy taxation.

Need for private investment

The German government had taken the first painful steps necessary to lift the east out of its economic depression. But more help was necessary if the region was ever to completely recover.

Privately owned businesses could provide that help. Companies from western Germany and around the world that were willing to build and invest in the east could go far to make up for thousands of failed enterprises. Money and support from these companies would not only produce new jobs and lift some of the burden of support off the government, it would provide assurance that better times were on the way. Discouraged easterners, seeing outsiders taking risks, might decide to give their region a second chance.

Finding businesses willing to invest in the region proved unexpectedly difficult. Treuhand red tape was the first obstacle. With over eight thousand businesses to be restructured, and more than a million claims on land and factories to be processed, the evaluation and sale process was depressingly slow. Birgit Breuel, who took over as Treuhand chief after former head Detlev Rohwedder was assassinated on April 1, 1991, re-

In April 1991, Birgit Breuel was named head of the Treuhand, the agency appointed to restructure the eastern German economy. Her predecessor had been assassinated by a Communist group.

mained confident in spite of national impatience. "There will be a very modern infrastructure here in five or six years," she promised.

Confusion over property rights was a second complication. Businesses had belonged to German citizens before the Communists took them in the late 1940s. Did those citizens now have the right to reclaim their property? Or had forty years and two changes in government erased those rights?

There were no hard and fast rules for the Treuhand to follow. Until the matter was settled, potential buyers were reluctant to make purchases for fear that ownership claims might prove troublesome and costly. As a result, the future of companies such as Ilka, a commercial refrigeration company in Dresden, hung in limbo.

Ilka's one claim to fame was the luge slide (similar to a bobsled run) they had built for the Calgary Olympics in 1988. Now over DM 88 million ($60 million) in debt and with no investors willing to risk an ownership battle, the company was doomed to bankruptcy.

Finally, in April 1991, the German justice system passed a law designed to save other companies from a fate such as Ilka's. The justices ruled that the Treuhand did not have to restore property seized by the Communists to a previous owner. Instead, that property could be sold to interested buyers. Monetary compensation would go to the previous owner at a later date, if necessary.

Big business goes east

With this legal hurdle out of the way, investment proceeded more briskly. Major automobile builders were some of the first to come into the region. This seemed only appropriate; eastern Germany's fascination with western cars had been apparent since the first days of reunification.

Volkswagen committed DM 5 billion to a new plant in Saxony in the south. Daimler-Benz began planning a truck plant near Berlin, while Opel opted to build cars in Thuringia.

Other industries came up with equally ambitious agendas. BASF, one of the country's "Big Three" chemical companies, invested DM 500 million in modernizing a plant in Brandenburg. Bayer, another chemical company, planned to spend the same amount on a new factory in Saxony-Anhalt.

A hopeful future

German industry was not the only one with a vision of what the east would someday become. The Coca-Cola Company had invested over DM 800 million in the region in 1989. It boasted that its newly trained eastern employees had already sold seventy-two million cases of the soft drink by 1992. "Low-calorie brands weren't very popular at first, but now, I can't keep enough of them in stock," exulted one store manager. McDonald's planned to achieve a similar triumph with one hundred new restaurants by the year 2000.

Other companies from France, the Netherlands, and Austria began moving in. British investment bankers lent money to promising new eastern German businesses specializing in construction and road building. Giant Luxembourg steelmaker Arbed S.A. invested over DM 200 million in eastern Germany with the goal of creating one of Europe's most modern steel plants.

Although initially Arbed needed only 620 workers (the former company in East Germany had employed over 6,000), it planned to produce as much steel as had the previous owner. Even more important, it would attract support industries—companies that manufactured parts and equipment, provided raw materials, and trans-

ported the finished product. All would offer new job opportunities.

A renewal of small businesses pointed to a hopeful German future as well. Between unification and the summer of 1992, over 1,350 existing companies were taken over and reshaped by enterprising business people, many of them easterners, who believed in the products their companies made.

Many of the businesses had been rejected by the Treuhand as too risky, and were scheduled for permanent closure. One example was Technische Gummiwaren, a rubber company that had been operating for over one hundred years. Michael Zack, its forty-two-year-old manager, knew that few German companies produced the specialized medical equipment that Technische did. He believed he could make the business a success if he could find markets for the goods.

Once confusing legal obstacles were resolved by the German government, many Western corporations such as the American F.W. Woolworth department store chain moved into eastern Germany.

Zack needed to get financing from the Treuhand to purchase the company, but even under the best terms available, he would come out of the deal with personal debts totaling a breathtaking DM 1.5 million. The Treuhand was concerned about granting him loans. Zack might be hardworking and sincere, but he had not budgeted for emergencies. Many other small companies had already failed for that very reason. Finally, both parties agreed on a lease-to-own plan.

"This company survived two world wars. I don't see why it shouldn't be able to survive socialism too," Zack observed.

Showplace of tomorrow

The east was changing, but in the face of enormous economic disruption, improvement was almost insignificant. Still, some easterners were encouraged. They believed the region would one

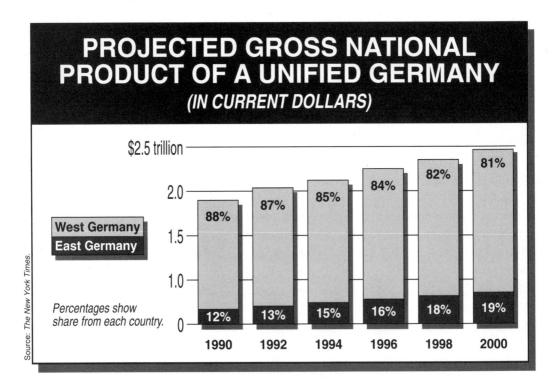

PROJECTED GROSS NATIONAL PRODUCT OF A UNIFIED GERMANY
(IN CURRENT DOLLARS)

West Germany
East Germany

Percentages show share from each country.

Source: The New York Times.

day become a showplace of ultra-modern technology. To prove it, they pointed to newly installed computerized banking systems that left the west's pre-electronic banks far behind.

"The East will eventually become as technically advanced as the West and in some cases even more so, since it will be getting the very latest in equipment," predicted Claus Schnabel of the German Economic Institute.

But how long would that advancement take? The economic depression was too deep-rooted to disappear with the coming of a few businesses. Change might be on the way, but too slowly for most. The east looked forward to nothing but years of hard times and sacrifice. The west watched a stream of Deutsche marks flowing out of their pockets and into the bottomless pit of reunification. German unhappiness was equalled only by German anger with Helmut Kohl and his policies. Kohl, the architect of reunification, had everything to lose if the days and months ahead proved too grim.

5

New Policies, Old Fears

"HELMUT, HELMUT!" THE happy crowds in Leipzig had chanted on a December day in 1990. Hundreds of thousands had turned out to honor Helmut Kohl, the hero of reunification, the man who promised to rescue them from the brink of disaster.

Four months later, their voices were less adoring. April elections had spelled defeat for many of Kohl's colleagues in the Christian Democratic Union, a sure sign that the chancellor's unification policies were highly unpopular. In Leipzig, a crowd seventy thousand strong turned out again to fill the same plaza. "Liar!" they roared every time Kohl's name was mentioned. "Pig!"

The hero had become the villain. The plan that had held such promise was now seen as a punishment. What had changed in so short a time?

The unification chancellor

(Opposite page) A German protestor conveys her opinion of German chancellor Helmut Kohl, the architect of Germany's reunification. As economic hardships persisted, Kohl's popular support dwindled.

Before 1989, few would have cast balding and bespectacled Helmut Kohl in the role of hero. Born in Ludwigshafen in southwest Germany in 1930, his stable, low-key political career began there in 1959. After competently serving as chairman of the Christian Democratic Union and as a

West German chancellor Helmut Kohl became known as "the unification chancellor" for his proposal that East and West Germany become one nation again. He was at first hailed as a hero, then later blamed when the many difficulties of reunification became apparent.

member of the Bundestag (the lower house of parliament), he was elected chancellor of West Germany in October 1982.

For seven years, Kohl went quietly about the business of strengthening ties between his country and the United States, forging new links with France, and promoting better relations with East Germany. At six-foot-four, he towered physically over many of his fellow officeholders, but few recognized him as a diplomatic giant.

Then in the early nineties, Kohl's leadership skills blossomed. Almost single-handedly he performed the impossible, overcoming objections to unification from European leaders, easing the Soviet Union's worries over the loss of an ally (East Germany), and amassing support from his own people. A landslide vote of approval in March 1990 cemented his plans for the two countries. Helmut Kohl went down in history as the "unification chancellor."

Conflicting expectations

Kohl had taken into account the fact that eastern and western reunification goals were diverse, that neither side would be entirely satisfied with the outcome of the project.

Westerners, satisfied with their comfortable lives, had long dreamed of unification for nationalistic and nostalgic reasons. They wanted to erase the division caused by World War II, and they wanted to proceed with little fuss or bother. Ideally, the end product would be a larger copy of the old Federal Republic, filled with western goods, laws, and values.

Easterners, accustomed to a severe socialist economy, wanted the freedom to attain western luxuries. With no clear understanding of democracy or market economy, easterners naively hoped to keep Communist-era benefits (low prices, guar-

"FIRST YOU GO TO THE BALL AND MARRY THE RICH PRINCE. THEN YOUR PUMPKIN TURNS INTO A MERCEDES - BENZ."

anteed jobs, and so on) while gaining the instant wealth they believed Kohl's plan promised. Some called this belief "Mercedes democracy."

Despite contradictory expectations, Kohl passionately believed that the fall of Communism was "a one-time historical chance" for reunification. In his enthusiasm, he promised his people that the hardships would be bearable. Costs would be contained. His pledge to impose no new taxes made the whole project sound almost painless.

In a matter of months, however, those promises had been broken. Shock gave way to anger when German citizens became aware of the enormous sacrifices they would be asked to make. They blamed Kohl, who had sold them on the project. Kohl had promised them a nation that would be bigger, stronger, and richer. Instead their hopes had been dashed. "Bigger" now seemed to apply

Youthful protestors march against government economic policies. Many had received their "red card," the German equivalent of a "pink slip," meaning they had lost their jobs. The sign reads "Give Kohl a red card!"

only to the size of the problems that Kohl had laid upon their shoulders.

Kohl had badly underestimated the size and complexity of reunification, as well as the people's support for the project. As he and his cabinet ministers dealt with those miscalculations, they also faced other problems that ranged from internal political division to Communist crimes, from domestic affairs to foreign policy concerns.

Divisions in government

During his years as chancellor, Helmut Kohl had successfully headed a ruling group or coalition made up of his own conservative party, the Christian Democratic Union (CDU), its sister party, the Christian Social Union, and the small, liberal Free Democratic party. The opposing Social Democrats, one of the largest and oldest parties in the country, had dropped in popularity and ranked second to the CDU.

The Free Democrats had gone along with the chancellor's policy-making while his public popularity remained high. But as reunification pressures caused that popularity to plummet, cracks began to form in the coalition. Criticism from Social Democrats became stronger as well. Almost every issue—immigration, health care, even the speed at which reunification was taking place—produced endless party wrangling. Decision making slowed and sometimes stalled completely.

Gerhard Stoltenberg, Kohl's minister of defense, resigned over policy disputes within Kohl's coalition party.

For the first time in a decade, Kohl encountered serious discord in his cabinet. Defense Minister Gerhard Stoltenberg and Foreign Minister Hans-Detrich Genscher resigned. Attempts to find replacements triggered more bickering.

Kohl was left with a double problem: to find creative answers to almost impossible reunification problems, and then to convince his opponents that those answers were best for the country. Most of the time, both appeared to be equally impossible tasks.

The *Stasi*

One of the responsibilities of Kohl's government after reunification was to bring untried Communist criminals—past leaders, secret police, and informers—to justice.

Investigation of the notorious *Staatsicherheit* (Ministry of State Security or *Stasi*) had begun months before, when impatient and angry demonstrators had stormed its headquarters, a beige concrete building in eastern Berlin. The crowds had climbed barricades and forced open doors. Finally they reached the secret files that revealed the extent of the organization's intrusion into private lives.

Folders on citizens suspected of anti-Communist beliefs and activities totalled over six million (one-third of the East German population) and filled miles of shelves. Additional reports were everywhere—helter-skelter on the floor, baled and tied with twine, stuffed unsorted into canvas bags. "They were drowning in their own paper," said Werner Fischer, a former dissident who supervised the files after they were opened.

The Committee to Dissolve the National Security was formed to investigate and shut down the organization. The committee confirmed earlier East German government reports: the *Stasi* had

consisted of 85,000 regular employees and over 100,000 secret informers who had tapped telephones, steamed open letters, and followed suspects in classic spy style. Government reports had also revealed 200,000 pistols, a fleet of cars, and thousands of telephone lines (an unbelievable number in a country where fewer than one in every three households owned a telephone).

Before the investigation was complete, *Stasi* treachery was revealed to have reached all levels of society. Members of the legislature were horrified to discover that fifty-six of their four hundred members had worked for the *Stasi* in some capacity. East Germany's first elected prime minister, Lothar de Maiziere, suspected for months of being a *Stasi* informant, could not brush away this fresh evidence and resigned.

In spite of overwhelming evidence, few of-

Former head of East Germany Erich Honecker (right) shakes the hand of former chief of the East German security forces Erich Mielke at the trial of former Communist leaders in 1992.

fenders faced criminal prosecution. Only five hundred former informants, those tied to schemes involving fraud or personal gain, were charged. Even *Stasi* head, eighty-three-year-old Erich Mielke, was spared. He was judged incompetent to stand trial by reason of senility.

Proof of *Stasi* involvement brought its own punishment, however. Uninvolved citizens scorned those who had collaborated with the secret police. Revelations of treachery spelled the end of careers, friendships, even marriages. Heinrich Fink, mild-mannered dean of theology at Humboldt University in Berlin, was dismissed

During a march to protest human rights abuses by the former Communist regime, East German demonstrators carry a picture of former East German leader Erich Honecker depicting him as a prison inmate.

when it was proved he had informed on students and colleagues. Dissident Wolfgang Schnur watched his newly formed opposition party, Democratic Awakening, nearly collapse after he was exposed as an informant. Knud Wollenberger fled to escape the anger of his activist wife and her friends on whom he had spied.

Communist crimes

As the *Stasi* investigation continued, the government began dealing with former Communist leaders, calling to account those who had committed abuses during their years of power.

Erich Honecker, leader of the former East Germany, was first on the list. He was charged with having issued the "shoot to kill" orders that resulted in the deaths of hundreds of escaping East Germans. Honecker fled the country before he could be brought to justice. After returning to Germany in 1992, he was diagnosed as being in the final stages of liver cancer and was released to spend the last months of his life in exile in Chile.

Former defense minister Heinz Kessler, former prime minister Willi Stoph, and two other ex-leaders, Fritz Streletz and Hans Albrecht, were charged with manslaughter. They, too, had al-

Demonstrators tore down paintings of Erich Honecker (left) and former Soviet president Leonid Brezhnev from the walls of the state police headquarters in East Berlin. A young man reads a sign placed in front of the pictures that calls the two Communist leaders "snoopers" and "parasites."

legedly issued shoot-to-kill orders in the past. East German border guards, who had earlier received medals, bonuses, and extra vacation time for killing escapees, were brought to trial as well.

Roughly half of the twenty-six former Politburo members (the executive committee of the Communist party) were investigated for possible treason, corruption, and abuse of power. Other leaders, like their *Stasi* comrades, were punished by the force of public opinion.

Unable to find work because of his past ties, one Communist party chief became a dishwasher at Berlin's Grand Hotel. A former army general lost both position and pride. "I live on the fourth floor in a three-room apartment with oven heating," he confessed. "I carry the coal up myself."

Although most who were formally tried received light sentences, some Germans deplored what they feared was "a spirit of vengeance" in bringing the offenders to justice. They remembered the Nuremberg Trials and the punishments that were judged overly harsh by some.

But most believed that these crimes should be paid for, that all those who had sacrificed their lives over the years should be avenged. "There can be no amnesty. For [Germany's] psychological and political health, it is necessary that those murderers are sentenced to at least a year or two," pronounced political scientist Michael Wolffsohn.

Domestic issues

The host of domestic concerns that Kohl and his government had to deal with were perhaps not as crucial to the country as creating jobs or dealing with Communist crimes. However, many of them were as important to the German people as any of the "larger" issues.

A union leader addresses a huge crowd of workers demonstrating against massive unemployment in former East Germany.

Choosing the site for the capital of Germany sparked heated debate across the country. Should the government remain in Bonn, "provisional capital" for forty-two years, or move back to Berlin, the former capital? Weeks of discussion resulted in compromise. The chancellor, the Bundestag, and key officials would make the move while thousands of lesser bureaucrats would continue to govern from Bonn.

Abortion was an issue of great interest to the east. East Germany's abortion policy had been one of the most liberal in the world. Eastern women continually protested the west's policy of strict limitation, which was to be imposed on them after a short transition period. In answer to their demands, the Bundestag finally passed a

East German women protest at the western border about becoming subject to West Germany's stricter abortion laws.

compromise bill, relaxing the law to allow greater numbers of abortions, while still keeping certain restrictions.

Demands for educational reform were just as vigorous but not as readily answered. Many state-run schools had been closed in the east; teachers accustomed to including Communist doctrine in their curriculum needed retraining before they could teach again. Western schools, filled to capacity before reunification, were seriously overcrowded with easterners seeking quality educations. The country badly needed money to set up new education and retraining programs. Kohl's government managed to set aside DM 7 billion to meet the most urgent needs. Since other demands inflated the reunification budget, any further aid would be years away.

Reorganizing defense

The fate of the former East German army was another issue that promised to burden the budget. The future of over ninety thousand soldiers plus endless numbers of Soviet-made ships, tanks, planes, and jeeps needed to be determined as soon as possible; money going to pay salaries and storage charges could be put to better use elsewhere.

Dealing with the troops was relatively easy. Many were integrated into the west's armed forces; others were offered early retirement. Getting rid of equipment was harder. The Soviets, with their pinched economy and new arms-control treaties, would not buy back equipment. Germany's defense department was left to find markets for what it could sell. The rest went for scrap, at an expense the government could ill afford; taking apart one battle tank could cost as much as DM 58,500 ($36,000).

As Kohl and his government concentrated on

PREWAR GERMANY

COLD WAR

REUNIFIED GERMANY

the future and its problems, world leaders remembered Germany's past. Its aggressive pride in homeland and race had led it into two wars. Would that nationalistic feeling resurface now that the country was whole and free of the watchful eye of the Allies? Germany had agreed to never again pose a military threat to world peace, but would it honor that agreement?

Some believed it might not. They argued that Germany, now the largest and richest country in Europe, might try to dominate its neighbors in more subtle ways. For instance, Germany had already pressured other European leaders to recognize the new Yugoslav republics of Croatia and Slovenia. It had urged that European Community (E.C.) meetings use German as well as English and French.

In a later move, the powerful German central bank, Deutsche Bundesbank, controller of German monetary policy and anchor of European economic stability, had adjusted its interest rates without warning. The effect on other European monetary systems was upsetting.

Many saw these moves as proof of their worst fears. "Germany is reflecting its power," observed one member of London's Royal Institute of International Affairs.

"Indisputably, Germany is going to occupy a totally dominant position in the years to come," stated Professor Simon Petermann of Brussels Free University.

An unlikely threat

Most leaders agreed that a unified Germany would be a more important participant in future world politics, but they thought it an unlikely threat to world order. They remembered Foreign Minister Genscher's assurances before reunification ceremonies had taken place:

We want to use [our] enhanced [political and economic] weight not to seek more power but to exercise more responsibility. We want German policy following unification to be a policy of the good example. We want to set that good example in the building of the European Community (EC). . . . We also want to set a good example in protecting the environment and strengthening the United Nations.

Long-term German actions spoke even louder than words. Since 1958, the country had been a responsible member of the European Community, a group that also included Great Britain, Ireland, France, Portugal, Spain, Italy, Greece, Denmark, the Netherlands, Belgium, and Luxembourg. Originally founded after World War II to help rebuild war-battered economies, the EC's aim for the 1990s was monetary, political, and economic union. The result was intended to be a unified Europe, more stable and prosperous than ever before.

Kohl was an outspoken champion of European unity. He and his people showed no interest in disputing boundaries or building empires as their ancestors had once done. Rather, they worked for the common good, pledging almost DM 18 billion ($11 billion) in support of the Persian Gulf War in 1991, and promising more support to emerging nations of the former Soviet Union and Communist bloc countries than any other country in the world.

As Genscher reemphasized, "We will demonstrate by our actions that German unification does not create a problem but rather helps to resolve other problems."

6

The Invisible Wall

NO GERMAN WOULD ever forget the cold November midnight when the Berlin Wall fell. In the hours before dawn, east and west had come together as long-lost friends, as partners in a dream come true, as family that vowed never to endure separation again.

"It's amazing how warmly we were greeted," an East German student recalled. "They cried. They were just as happy as we were."

Yet almost before the celebration ended and the last sip of champagne was swallowed, tension had begun to build between the two sections of the country. Misunderstandings developed. Tempers flared. By the time unification became official in October 1990, an invisible barrier of suspicion and resentment divided the nation.

The challenges to reunification were more than economic and political. Over the past forty years, enormous differences in values and viewpoints had developed between the two countries. Hard-hit easterners were unprepared, socially and emotionally, for life in a free society.

(Opposite page) In November 1989 eager East Germans crowd West Berlin's shopping district on the first weekend after the east-west border restrictions were lifted.

Differing values

The future of the new Germany would be determined by how rapidly both sides learned to respect their differences, and how well easterners

87

adapted to the challenges of their new world.

Reunification brought together two nations that were, for all intents and purposes, opposites. West Germans were modern and fast-paced. They wanted to look good, feel good, and "have it all." Though they were well on the way to achieving those goals, they were often dissatisfied. Frustrated by a less than perfect world, they were driven to improve, to achieve, to try different things. "Even in leisure, we are not particularly at ease," admitted one western businessperson.

In the GDR, Communist control had deprived easterners of contact with the ever-changing Western world. Life-styles were decades behind the West. Easterners had learned that life was smooth and secure as long as every part of it conformed to Communist rules and regulations. They hid their unhappiness and left complaints unspoken. Questioning authority was as dangerous as trying to leave the country.

An East German man shovels coal for his home from a pile dumped in the street for public use. The scene exemplifies the comparative backwardness of the eastern lifestyle prior to reunification.

Faced with a more restricted way of life, easterners learned to appreciate the few things they had. They relied on each other. Simplicity was valued above sophistication, friendship above competition, group solidarity over individual achievement.

When asked to sacrifice these qualities in the western scramble for success, they were indignant. "Before, if you had a friend in trouble, you'd cover for him at work and it would be OK. . . . Now it's everybody for himself. I ask myself, 'Is that progress?'" grumbled one middle-aged parking lot attendant.

Western scorn

Armed with opposing sets of values, the two sides were bound to clash as they came together under the most difficult of situations—the melding of two countries into one.

Western sympathy and support for the east's plight became patronizing, then resentful, as everything eastern—industry, business, merchandise, and standard of living—fell short of western standards. *Ossis* (unflattering slang for easterners) were obviously careless and unskilled. They could not do anything right, whether it was managing the environment or building a workable automobile.

Westerners pointed out that easterners constantly whined about their troubles but waited for someone else to solve them. The lazy *Ossis* wanted the good life, but they did not want to work for it. If reunification succeeded, it would be because of western support, western ingenuity, and western money.

Easterners, standing in the ruins of their society, disliked the west's overbearing attitude. *Wessis* (slang for westerners) treated them like second-class citizens, expecting exaggerated gratitude for every Deutsche mark sent east. *Wessis* imposed new laws, life-styles, and values without a second thought for the customs, beliefs, and expectations they trampled upon in the process.

Barbel Bohley, founder of the New Forum party, explained some of the east's frustration:

> For half a century we have not been allowed to decide for ourselves what we want. In the old days, whenever we asked why things had to be done a certain way, we were told, "Because that's the way they are done in the glorious Soviet state." Now, since reunification, we're told that we have to do everything the way it was done in West Germany.

That underlying frustration caused anger to bubble up over little things as well. Easterners noted that *Wessis* seldom came to the east without pointing out to visitors how grim and shabby conditions were. On other rare occasions, they came for the bargains they could find.

Eastern frustration

One eastern Berliner complained, "They are unbelievably arrogant. They have plenty of money, but they come over here because everything is cheaper. They behave as if everything belongs to them, as if they know it all and we are stupid."

Signs of hostility were everywhere. Westerners muttered curses at the pollution-spewing Trabants when easterners headed west for a day of shopping. In eastern Berlin, graffiti announced, "Berlin must stay red." A T-shirt urged, "Rebuild the wall—two meters higher."

Frustration was greatest for German youth in both sections of the country. They did not remember "the old days" before Communist rule. They found it difficult to justify the sacrifices they were making to bring together two countries that had, for them, always been separate.

One student at Bonn University explained:

For me, the east is like Austria. There they speak German too. But I feel no tie—I have no sense that eastern Germans are my countrymen. Older people feel this connection more, because they lived through the division. I grew up with the fact the GDR was another country. I think this is typical for my generation.

Eastern Germans had never dreamed that reunification would bring division, frustration, and resentment. The discovery left them disillusioned. So did freedom itself. Living in a democracy was not as carefree or rewarding as they had imagined. Adjusting socially and emotionally was difficult. For some, it seemed almost impossible.

Loss of social benefits, long taken for granted under communism, came as a shock to everyone.

Gone were crime-free neighborhoods, free child care, and after-school clubs that kept teens off the streets.

Gone, too, were government-sponsored athletic programs, notorious for unethical practices, but appreciated for the luxuries they had offered. Children chosen to train in any of the twenty-three sports schools across the country were paid a monthly wage from the age of ten years on. Adults earned a salary at least 50 percent higher than the ordinary worker. The best athletes were given opportunities to travel outside the country. In addition, they had the chance to gain fame and show off East Germany's devotion to athletes in competitions such as the Olympic Games. Now these fringe benefits were no longer available to German families.

Financial mismanagement

As old benefits disappeared, new difficulties arose to take their places. One problem, coping with the pain of financial mismanagement, was a major concern for thousands of easterners.

For decades, the Communist government had overseen and regulated all eastern money matters. Personal bank accounts had been strictly controlled. Loans were granted only if the government decided they were necessary and prudent. Interest rates were low.

All that changed with reunification. Suddenly, easterners were at liberty to purchase what they chose. Many ignored consumer advice centers that warned of the responsibilities and hazards of western finance, especially loans and credit cards. Thousands of families spent beyond their means, then sank deeply into debt, even bankruptcy.

Rolf Schreiber (his name has been changed to protect his privacy) was one of that number. Schreiber had enjoyed his newfound liberty by going on several shopping sprees to western Berlin. A budget was the last thing on his mind. Using credit, he purchased home furnishings, a luxury video recorder, a seldom-used microwave oven.

In no time at all, Schreiber lost track of how much he had spent. Then, a layoff notice arrived from the firm at which he had worked. Unemployed and uncertain about where he had gone wrong, Schreiber passed the empty days drinking beer and worrying. With trembling hands, he sorted through the drawerful of bills he had no hope of repaying, and asked, "What can I do?"

Not everyone spent their way into debt, but all worried about what tomorrow would bring. Un-

Consumers check out East German canned goods that are on sale. After the currency union in July 1990, most East German shops refused to sell East German goods. Factories were forced to sell directly to consumers at a substantial discount.

certainty was exceptionally painful for a people used to having their lives spelled out for them from cradle to grave.

Entrepreneurs feared that their businesses would fail. Senior citizens wondered if they would be edged out of the new welfare system. "My mother is afraid," admitted one worker. "She will retire soon, and she worries that she will never get her pension."

Parents fretted that their families would be penniless before better times returned. "We're all going to end up in the streets," predicted a pessimistic worker in the city of Schwerin. "My son has lost his job, but my wife still naively believes things will get better. Not me."

From despair to violence

Most eastern Germans did their best to go forward regardless of the insurmountable problems they faced. Others seemed unable to adjust.

Suicide rates rose, especially in people over age fifty-five who had been forced into early retirement. "At that age, what do you do when you suddenly discover you don't have any worth anymore?" one easterner asked.

Some people expressed their feelings through bloodshed and terrorism. Their actions reflected negative feelings that had been suppressed too long—anger at the Communists who had destroyed their world, despair that the west was taking so long to put it back together again.

"The lid is off now," observed one psychotherapist, referring to the removal of Communist authority that had controlled easterners' every action and reaction. "The repressed violence can escape. It will get worse because of new social problems—a crisis of identity, of confidence, of authority, and of security."

Immigration

Germany's liberal refugee policy fed the fires of anger and resentment. The Federal Republic of Germany, remorseful for atrocities committed against Jews and others during World War II, had stated in its constitution that all foreigners suffering political persecution could find protection in Germany. "All it takes is one word of German—*asyl* [political asylum]," a member of Kohl's cabinet explained. Refugees could then enter the country and remain until their case histories were reviewed, often a matter of months.

In the past, the issue of asylum had not been controversial. From 1948 until 1989, many refugees to the west were East Germans, fleeing Communist oppression. The FRG welcomed them. The economy was growing, and there were not enough workers to fill new positions.

The tide had swollen in 1989, gathering force

from the arrival of ethnic Germans from Poland, Romania, and the Soviet Union. Again, the Bonn government did nothing to stem the flow. It believed that with time and an economic upturn in the east, a balance would be achieved that would slow the movement.

But the 1990s brought a new stream of outsiders. This time they came from Croatia, Romania, and war-torn Bosnia, from Africa, even from India. Although most did not qualify to stay in the country, food, housing, and jobs were provided until each individual situation could be evaluated. The cost of these social services placed an added strain on the already overloaded budget.

As reunification made its impact on living conditions, xenophobia (fear or hatred of foreigners) and acts of violence grew. Unemployed Germans blamed "outsiders" for taking jobs and welfare benefits, attacking long-term Turkish residents as well as recent refugees.

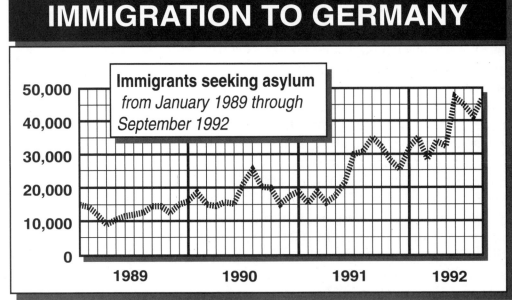

IMMIGRATION TO GERMANY

Immigrants seeking asylum *from January 1989 through September 1992*

50,000
40,000
30,000
20,000
10,000
0

1989   1990   1991   1992

Source: German Interior Ministry, German Office for Protection of the Constitution.

German riot police arrest violent demonstrators who attacked an asylum for foreign refugees. Many Germans, feeling frustrated by economic hardships, vented their anger on immigrants they believed were unfairly taking jobs and supplies needed by citizens.

In answer to the violence, Interior Minister Rudolf Seiters banned the radical right-wing group, Nationalist Front, responsible for many of the attacks. He also began a crackdown on other radical parties that had been allowed to form again after 1964. Statistics showed that membership in these groups had increased by 25 percent between 1990 and 1993. Their viewpoint was expressed by one fifteen-year-old Berliner who boldly stated, "Everything wasn't exactly right [during Hitler's Third Reich], but there was order in Germany. Then there were just Germans in Germany. I don't like the way Germany looks now."

While the interior minister tried to control the

Thousands march through Berlin's famous Brandenburg Gate to protest the growing air of fascism and anti-Semitism in the reunified nation.

flames of hatred, Chancellor Kohl addressed the problem from a different angle. He called for constitutional reforms that would curb liberal entrance provisions for foreigners.

Social Democrats initially opposed the move, but their opposition weakened as the attacks escalated. Armed with the promise of reforms, Kohl hastened to reassure the world that German doors remained open to those in need.

"If people are persecuted on political, racial, or religious grounds, they can still come here any time. This constitutional guarantee will not be changed."

Anti-Semitism

As disturbing as attacks on "outsiders" was a rebirth of anti-Semitism (a hatred of Jewish people) that had infected Germany in the past. During one violent incident, agitators toppled a monument that honored the thousands of Berlin Jews killed in the Holocaust. Anti-Jewish slogans were found scribbled on walls. Fires were set at former concentration camps where over six million Jews had been murdered during World War II.

Western Germans had hoped that anti-Semitism no longer existed in their country. During the years after World War II, they had searched their consciences, condemned their Nazi past, and tried to teach their children tolerance for all.

East Germans had not. In the 1950s, the Communists had announced that East Germans were not responsible for Nazi crimes committed during the war. Not until spring of 1990 did the GDR's parliament confess shame and grief over past

Neo-Nazi "skinheads" shouting Sieg Heil! *and giving the Nazi salute march in Leipzig to protest the influx of non-white, non-German peoples into Germany.*

atrocities and ask "the Jews in all the world for forgiveness."

That government action had little effect on deeply ingrained eastern attitudes. When asked about the Holocaust, some easterners pretended that the shameful episode had never taken place. Others insisted that Communists, trade unionists, and homosexuals had been equally victimized by the Nazis.

As old prejudices reappeared, the Jewish community, especially in eastern Germany, expressed concern. Older people, remembering the past, watched the unrest grow and debated leaving the region. The younger generation argued that offenders made up a tiny portion of the population, and that the government would never let the threat get out of hand.

To protest the recent right-wing attacks on foreigners, people of color, and Jews, German citizens in Bonn march with a banner proclaiming "Stop the establishment of the Fourth Reich!"

Klaus Gysi, retired minister of culture in the east and also a Jew, acknowledged the tremendous differences between Kohl's government and that of Hitler's Nazi party in the 1930s. Nevertheless, he argued that the menace could not be ignored. "Anti-Semitism in Germany will always be a danger. . . . The German [race] can never be allowed to forget what it has done."

A new identity

As easterners struggled with the burdens of reunification, many looked back on the past with a kind of nostalgia. The years of communism had been terrible. No one wanted to live under that oppressive system again. But at least those years had been relatively well ordered, secure, and stable. Easterners had been proud of their accomplishments. There had been no disdainful *Wessis* making them feel inferior.

From the memory of "the good old days," an unexpected eastern identity began to take shape.

Berlin Jews and other protestors stand watch in front of the Sachsenhausen concentration camp, preserved from World War II as a memorial. The camp had been firebombed by a neo-Nazi group.

An upsurge in the sale of eastern-made products signaled its birth. Eastern beer, toothpaste, sour pickles, and even liquid detergents such as *Fit*—long hated by East German women—all began to sell at an astonishing rate.

"I think . . . that people say to themselves, 'If the quality is OK, why should I buy a western product and endanger an eastern job?'" a soap company executive explained.

But there was more to the movement than that. Easterners had begun to take pride again in who they were and where they came from. They were rediscovering value in their old life-styles. "At present it's still wispy and diffuse, but the search for a separate identity is now in full swing," stated one expert on east-west differences.

A preference for eastern merchandise was not the sole expression of the new identity. Former East German customs and traditions, such as the *Jugendweihe*, a coming-of-age ceremony instituted by the Communists, regained popularity. Numerous families chose to observe this celebration along with or in preference to Christian confirmations or Jewish bar mitzvahs.

Recovering eastern self-esteem

Eastern-oriented political groups also gained support. "After the great hopes of 1990, many people in the new German states now feel that they are . . . unwelcome politically, economically, socially, and culturally," stated the founders of one such group. Its leaders believed that their organization, and others like it, would give easterners a stronger voice in representing their region in the future.

The development of a new German identity was a sign of recovering eastern self-esteem. At the same time, many experts worried that it was one more brick in the invisible wall that grew higher with each passing day. As one sociologist pointed out, "We were all Germans together, and we thought we would be able to understand each other perfectly. But now we realize that the influence of western values here, and of Stalinism there, created differences that will last a long time."

The rift would remain until both sides forgot at least a portion of their differences. Reunification would not be complete until more Germans remembered that they had once been partners in realizing a dream.

INTERCLUB ERFURT
Haus am Breitstrom

7

A New Germany: Finishing the Work

"JOYFUL AT THE outset, the unification of Germany has become a process of painful realization."

These words, written by Herbert Henzler, management consultant and German university professor, probably express the sentiments of most Germans. The past years have been problem-filled. Improvement often seems insignificant—an "open" sign in the window of a struggling business, or the report of shorter lines at unemployment bureaus.

The "painful realization" includes an awareness that many more problems wait to be addressed. German citizens wonder impatiently when the ruined eastern economy will begin to rebound. Some question whether their leaders have a clear vision for the country's future. Others look within themselves and ask whether the German people have the wisdom to cooperate and find compromises to their differences.

To the casual observer, the eastern economic scene looks much the same as it did in 1990. The

(Opposite page) Students in Erfurt, an eastern German city, take a break from classes at an organization that retrains adults for new careers.

economy, after following a long downward spiral, remains on the brink of ruin. Some 40 percent of the eastern German work force are unemployed or in government make-work programs. Without help from the west, eastern citizens would be penniless.

Despite continuing tough times, some easterners now believe that the worst of their reunification woes are over. "People feel they're about to bounce back, and this is tremendously motivating," reported one official.

This cautious optimism is not unfounded. Although experts are quick to point out that the eastern German economy will not achieve real stability until after the turn of the century, hints of improvement abound. Telephone crews installed more telephones in the first year of reunification than during all the decades of Communist rule. Colorful neon signs light up formerly gray streets. Flowers bloom in window boxes.

More importantly, private investment has al-

Workers repair and renovate the inadequate and outmoded East German telephone system on the east side of Berlin. More telephones were installed in the east in the first year of reunification than in four decades of Communist rule.

most tripled from DM 26 billion in 1991 to DM 72 billion in 1992. Increased investment should lead to new jobs, counterbalancing additional business closures by the Treuhand. Demands for unemployment support may soon lessen as the economy begins to grow.

Eastern German grocery shoppers delight in the new availability of fresh produce, previously a rare commodity.

Changing expectations

A great deal of the responsibility for improvement rests with the government, but even more important is the attitude of the German people themselves. In view of the differences separating the country, critics question whether the people can summon the patience and tolerance needed to let the process work.

The national mood is not reassuring. Anger and disappointment continue to drive a wedge between easterners and westerners. Right wing, neo-Nazi violence infuriates the majority of Germans, some of whom want to answer bloodshed with bloodshed.

Regardless of continued tension, experts predict that the German people will succeed. As proof, they cite a significant number of easterners who have adopted a western motto: work hard and gather the benefits later. Instead of complaining, citizens are rolling up their sleeves and rebuilding their lives. Many westerners, finding that higher taxes and social service cutbacks have not seriously changed their standard of living, have taken a wait-and-see attitude, hoping that the worst of their reunification troubles are over.

Another argument for success is German character itself. History records German pessimism.

German citizens march in protest of the killing of three Turks, ages 10, 15, and 50, by neo-Nazi extremists on November 22, 1992. Hate crimes by neo-Fascist groups infuriate most Germans, many of whom have personally suffered from the Nazi terror of Hitler's Third Reich.

"In our Fatherland, we grumble: every stupidity, everything that is wrong vexes us," wrote Heinrich Heine, a German philosopher, in 1828. But history also reveals the German tendency to succeed in spite of (or perhaps because of) that grumbling. Hardships appear to spark creativity and a willingness to sacrifice. As one German economist theorized, "Germans thrive on creative panic. It is when they are not worried that things are bad."

Germans might bicker and complain, but it is likely they will see the work through. In time, there is even the chance that they will share a common pride in their accomplishments.

The reunification project is well underway. Laws and guidelines are in place; committed leaders are attempting to promote strategies that will carry reunification on to completion.

But while progress is being made, some wonder if the existing plan is the best and shortest route to a promising future. Experts believe that corrections in economic, political, and social policies could help accelerate the process.

Economic corrections

Under the government's present policy of uniform development, money has been distributed fairly and equally across the east. In some locales—centers of business and industry like Leipzig and Berlin—the groggy economy is responding. In others such as Leuna, a small refinery town that relied on oil from the Soviet Union, the economy still falters.

Herbert Henzler and other management specialists believe that the government should adjust its existing policy by directing extra help to responsive districts.

"Instead of trying to 'smear' economic growth uniformly across the new federal states in the

Within a year of reunification, this formerly drab shop has been transformed into a colorful, well-stocked shoe store.

east, Germany should concentrate on those regional centers with an historic and proven expertise in specific industries," Henzler suggests. "We would see a flowering of optics and electronics work around Jena, printing in Leipzig, shipbuilding in Rostock, and chemicals in Halle."

The response to this action would eventually boost the economy of the entire country. One example of such regional development has already begun in the town of Unterwellenborn, where a powerful steel company began establishing itself shortly after reunification. Soon a recycling plant started operations nearby. Forecasting further economic growth, the government agreed to build a major highway through the area. Applications from other new businesses promise to turn the area into, as one observer called it, an "island of prosperity."

Henzler maintains that this same unequal distribution of funds could benefit higher education as well. The government has set aside limited money to spend on revitalizing and replacing universities and colleges that have been closed throughout the east. That money might be best directed into a few educational centers that could become intellectual and economic hubs of their regions, attracting talented people from across the nation. These centers could emphasize programs important for eastern improvement—urban renewal, transportation, and environmental research.

Flourishing academic centers would stimulate economic growth. So would incentives such as promotions and bonuses, offered to those willing

Students at a public school in eastern Germany. German leaders recognize the important role education plays in carrying reunification to completion.

to establish businesses on the "new frontier." Westerners moving east would not only help counterbalance movement out of the region, but could teach easterners the basics of a market-driven economy.

The risks for these new entrepreneurs cannot be denied. "You have to be something of a pioneer to come in here," Birgit Breuel, head of the Treuhand, admitted. But with qualified managers to boost productivity and enthusiasm, and with strong monetary support from parent companies in the west, that risk would be reduced.

Political corrections

Citizens in the east have complained of being overlooked and undervalued by German leadership since the early days of reunification. Their complaints have some basis. Prime ministers of three of the five eastern Länder are westerners. The east is poorly represented in the Bundestag; eastern politicians often cannot make their voices heard over those of the western majority.

One eastern deputy bemoaned this powerlessness after a legislative debate over the relocation of the German supreme court into the east. "Even though all Eastern deputies were united, from Democratic Socialists to Christian Democrats, we had no chance [against the west]. We lost by about 300 votes," he said bitterly.

German leadership must address these concerns if easterners are to develop feelings of loyalty to and confidence in their new country. Government must be more aware of the east's position on all issues, especially controversial ones. One positive example of this was the Bundestag's support of eastern demands to relocate the nation's capital from Bonn to Berlin.

Western political parties should include eastern concerns in their platforms. In so doing, they

might reduce eastern involvement in the right-wing and other special interest groups that are gaining in popularity.

Fair and responsible decision making will go far to overcome feelings of inferiority and resentment that have developed among easterners in recent years.

Social corrections

In order to heal the divisions that exist between the two sections of the country, social issues need to be more carefully addressed than in the past.

For the sake of their economic well-being, easterners must learn to admire and copy those who succeed in business, not regard them as thieves or capitalist exploiters as the Communists taught.

This adjustment will be particularly difficult,

A session of the Bundestag, the lower house of Germany's parliament. Eastern representation in the German government is still unsatisfactory to most easterners, who feel their voice is not always heard by the government.

A marker in the pavement on a bridge spanning the Werra River that once separated East from West Germany reads "Bridge of Unification."

given that many former Communist bosses are now managing businesses and making profits in the east. Rainer Potte is one such person. After reunification, Potte purchased the collective farm he once managed, transforming it into a cooperative that houses a dairy, a beverage distributor, a construction company, a restaurant, an auto repair shop, and a furniture store.

Public resentment has festered against Potte. "The [Communists] have stayed where they were before—at the top," complained one of his neighbors. Still, Potte's businesses, and others like them, contribute to the east's economic growth. They have provided jobs for dozens of people in the region. Easterners must understand that the person willing to take risks is often the person of most benefit to society.

Other eastern attitudes need reshaping if tensions are to be eased. Counseling will be vital to help easterners deal with feelings of hostility and despair, to help them replace long-held Communist beliefs and prejudices with more open attitudes.

Scornful western attitudes must be altered as well. Easterners need to feel that they are contributing to their country's recovery. Eastern talent and leadership should be recognized. Eastern values of friendship, loyalty, and thrift can help moderate the fast-paced, materialistic western society. The effort will go far to create a stronger, more balanced German identity.

Finishing the work

The new Germany is blessed with funds, expertise, and the stubborn will to succeed. Remolding the lives of millions of people is no easy task, but a majority of Germans are willing to continue until the work is finished. Their reunification dream is tarnished, but it survives.

Bishop Martin Kruse, former leader of the West German Protestant church, expresses a steadfast hope that is shared by millions: "What becomes of all this will be left to history and the hand of God. I am neither a prophet nor a politician, but I believe that we are growing together, not apart."

Glossary

Allies: The countries that joined in opposition to Germany, Japan, and Italy in World War II. They included Great Britain, France, the Soviet Union, and the United States.

anti-Semitism: Prejudice against Jews.

asylum: Protection offered by a sanctuary or refuge, or by one country to refugees from another country.

Basic Law: The constitution of West Germany.

Bundestag: The lower house of German parliament. Members of the Bundestag, elected by German citizenry, pass laws and elect the chancellor and president.

coalition: A temporary union of distinct parties, persons, or states for joint action.

communism: An economic system in which there is no private property, and the people as a group own the means for producing all goods.

demilitarize: To free from organized military control; to take away military power.

denazify: To rid of Nazi elements or influences.

dissident: One who disagrees.

economy: A system of producing, distributing, and consuming wealth.

European Community (also EC or European Economic Community)**:** A European common market formed in 1958 by Belgium, France, West Germany, Italy, Luxembourg, and the Netherlands to achieve closer economic ties. In 1973, Denmark, Ireland, and the United Kingdom joined.

fiscal: Financial; having to do with government treasury, such as income from taxes, licenses, and so on.

free-market economy: An economic system in which buying or selling can be carried on without restrictions on pricing or productivity.

immigrate: To come into a new country, region, or environment in order to settle there.

inflation: A continual increase in prices throughout a nation's economy. The rate of inflation generally goes up if prices rise more quickly than wages, or if wage increases exceed gains in productivity and an employer must charge higher prices to make up the difference. A rise in inflation reduces the value, or purchasing power, of money.

Länder: Regional division in Germany similar to states in the United States, each having its own constitution and government.

Mercedes democracy: The East German desire for democratic freedoms, motivated by economics more than politics.

nationalism: Devotion to one's country; patriotism. The belief that national interest and security are more important than international considerations.

NATO: North Atlantic Treaty Organization. An organization, formed in 1950, that provides unified military leadership for the common defense of sixteen Western nations, including the United States, Great Britain, France, and Germany.

Nazi party: The National Social German Workers' Party, founded in 1919 and abolished in 1945. Under Hitler, it seized control of Germany in 1933, systematically eliminated opposition, and put into effect its program of nationalism, racism, rearmament, and aggression.

neo-Nazi (literally, "new Nazi"): Any of a number of radical right-wing political parties that seek to reestablish Nazi principles, particularly white supremacy, anti-Semitism, and violence.

Ossis: Unflattering slang for eastern Germans.

perestroika: A Soviet term for political and economic restructuring, designed to move the Soviet Union closer to the market democracies of the West.

reparation: Compensation; anything paid or done to make up for a wrong or injury.

socialist: A supporter of socialism, the political system that places production and ownership in the hands of the state and discourages private ownership.

Solidarity party: An organization of Polish trade unions; the party headed the struggle that eventually led to economic and political reform in Poland.

Stasi: Staatsicherheit or Ministry of State Security. The much-hated Communist organization that helped control all aspects of East German life through its system of secret police and informers.

Treuhand: *Treuhandanstalt* or Trust Fund Institution. An organization set up by the German government to facilitate reunification; its responsibilities include evaluating former Communist-controlled businesses, offering them for sale to private businesspeople, making loans, and approving credit for new buyers.

unity bonds: Interest-bearing certificates, issued by the German government, to help finance the cost of reunification.

Warsaw Pact: A treaty, signed in Warsaw, Poland, in 1955, bringing the Communist nations of Europe under a unified military command led by the Soviet Union.

Wessis: Unflattering slang for western Germans.

xenophobia: A fear or hatred of strangers or foreigners.

Suggestions for Further Reading

Stephen Ashton, *The Cold War*. London: BT Batsford Ltd., 1990.

Richard Collier, *Bridge Across the Sky*. New York: McGraw-Hill, 1978.

Doris M. Epler, *The Berlin Wall: How It Rose and Why It Fell*. Brookfield, CT: The Millbrook Press, 1992.

Jim Hargrove, *The Story of the Unification of Germany*. Chicago: Children's Press, 1991.

Max Hastings, *Victory in Europe*. Boston: Little, Brown & Co., 1985.

Terry Tillman, *The Writings on the Wall*. Santa Monica, CA: 22/7 Publishing Co., 1990.

Works Consulted

Konrad Adenauer, *Memoirs 1945-53*. Chicago: Henry Regnery Company, 1965.

Daniel Benjamin, "Cracking Down on the Right," *Time*, December 14, 1992.

Daniel Benjamin, "Foreigners, Go Home!" *Time*, November 23, 1992.

Daniel Benjamin, "Wall of Shame," *Time*, November 20, 1989.

"Bonn Says *Ja* to Berlin," *Time*, July 1, 1991.

Stephen Budiansky, "And the Wall Came Tumbling Down," *U.S. World & News Report*, November 20, 1989.

Stephen Burant, ed., *East Germany: A Country Study*. (Prepared by the Federal Research Division of the Library of Congress) United States Government, 1988.

Audrey Choi, "Eastern German Manager Takes a Stab at Privatization," *The Wall Street Journal*, August 17, 1992.

Howard G. Chua-Eoan, "The Pain of Purification," *Time*, December 31, 1990.

George J. Church, "Freedom!" *Time*, November 20, 1989.

"The Costs Spiral," *Euromoney*, October 1990.

Kevin Cote, "Second Class Citizens in Their Own Country," *Advertising Age*, February 19, 1990.

Donald S. Detwiler, *Germany: A Short History*. Carbondale: Southern Illinois University Press, 1989.

"East Germans Swim River to Safety," *The Fresno Bee*, February 14, 1962.

"East Germany Ratifies Pact with Bonn," *The New York Times*, June 14, 1973.

John Elson, "Where Have the Commies Gone?" *Time*, July 8, 1991.

"A Farewell to Arms," *Time*, September 24, 1990.

Max Frankel, "U.S. Sending 1,500 Troops to Bolster West Berlin," *The New York Times*, August 19, 1961.

"From Heroes to Infamy," *Time*, September 16, 1991.

Mary Fulbrook, *A Concise History of Germany*. New York: Cambridge University Press, 1990.

David Gergen, "Make Way for Germany," *U.S. News & World Report*, October 21, 1991.

"Germany," *The Economist*, May 23, 1992.

"Helmut Gets Clobbered," *Time*, May 6, 1991.

William A. Henry III, "The Price of Obedience," *Time*, February 3, 1992.

Herbert Henzler, "Managing the Merger: A Strategy for the New Germany," *Harvard Business Review*, January/ February 1992.

Mildred Istona, "Voices from the New Germany," *Chatelaine*, February 1991.

James O. Jackson, "End of the Miracle," *Time*, May 18, 1992.

James O. Jackson, "Fear and Betrayal in the *Stasi* State," *Time*, February 3, 1992.

James O. Jackson, "The New Germany Flexes Its Muscles," *Time*, April 13, 1992.

James O. Jackson, "Unity's Shadows," *Time*, July 8, 1991.

Tamara Jones, "Bonn to Expel Thousands of Romanians, Gypsies," *Los Angeles Times*, September 18, 1992.

Karl Kaiser, "Germany's Reunification," *Foreign Affairs*, Winter 1991.

Frederick Kempe, "A Hint of Dawn," *The Wall Street Journal*, August 28, 1992.

Stephen Kinzer, "Group Is Formed to Defend East German Interests," *The New York Times*, July 12, 1992.

Stephen Kinzer, "One More Wall to Smash: Arrogance in the West," *The New York Times*, August 12, 1992.

Robin Knight, "Voting for a Change," *U.S. News & World Report*, March 19, 1990.

"Kohl: We Are Far from One Germany," *Business Week*, May 18, 1992.

Walecia Konrad, "The Real Thing Is Thundering Eastward," *Business Week*, April 13, 1992.

Charles Lane et al., "'Why Don't They Share?'" *Newsweek*, April 1, 1991.

Robert Emmet Long, ed., *The Reunification of Germany*. New York: The H.W. Wilson Company, 1992.

John Marks, "Germany's Heir Apparent," *U.S. News & World Report*, December 30, 1991.

David Marsh, *The Germans: A People at the Crossroads.* New York: St. Martin's Press, 1989.

Tyler Marshall, "Kohl Booed While Marking German Unity," *Los Angeles Times*, October 4, 1992.

Tyler Marshall, "New Wall Goes up in Germany," *Los Angeles Times*, August 20, 1992.

Thomas Mayer and Gunther Thumann, "Paving the Way for German Unification," *Finance & Development*, December 1990.

Michael Meyer, "The Myth of German Unity," *Newsweek*, July 9, 1990.

Michael Meyer et al., "'Is It Possible?'" *Newsweek*, November 20, 1989.

Drew Middleton, "West Germany Is Making Strides Toward Industrial Rehabilitation," *The New York Times*, January 4, 1950.

Bruce W. Nelan, "And Now There Is One," *Time*, October 8, 1990.

Bruce W. Nelan, "Kohl," *Time*, January 7, 1991.

Bruce W. Nelan, "Ode to a New Day," *Time*, October 15, 1990.

Mary Nemeth, "Slowing the Juggernaut," *Maclean's*, August 8, 1990.

"No Exit for Ex-Leaders," *Time*, June 3, 1991.

Rod Nordland and Carroll Bogert, "The Long Shadow," *Newsweek*, May 7, 1990.

Richard F. Nyrop, ed., *Federal Republic of Germany: A Country Study.* (Prepared by American University) United States Government, 1982.

Andreas Oldag, "Spending Their Way to Bankruptcy," *World Press Review*, December 1991.

Andrew Phillips, "A Vote for Unity," *Maclean's,* April 2, 1990.

Andrew Phillips, "Germany Reborn," *Maclean's*, March 19, 1990.

Ferdinand Protzman, "Germany to Turn Railways into Private Companies," *The New York Times*, July 16, 1992.

Sharon Reier, "Breaking with Big Brother," *Financial Weekly*, March 5, 1991.

John Rodden, "Lurching Toward Educational Reform: East Germany's 'Trabulations,'" *America*, October 26, 1991.

Luc Rosenzweig, "Germany Hopes to Set a 'Good Example,'" *World Press Review*, December 1990.

Ed Rubenstein, "The Economic Wall," *National Review*, December 22, 1989.

Gail E. Schares and John Templeman, "East Germany: Clinging to the Hard Line—And Taking a Hard Fall," *Business Week*, September 4, 1989.

"Selective Refuge," *Time*, December 21, 1992.

"Sentenced to Live," *Time*, January 25, 1993.

"A Sky-High Price for German Unity," *U.S. News & World Report*, February 25, 1991.

Louis L. Snyder, ed., *Documents of German History*. New Brunswick, NJ: Rutgers University Press, 1958.

Theo Sommer, "East Germany Then and Now," *World Press Review*, September 1986.

Douglas Stanglin, "Unhappily, into the Future," *U.S. News & World Report*, March 5, 1990.

Walter Sullivan, "Adenauer Pledges Bonn-Allied Aid to West Berlin in Any Emergency," *The New York Times*, May 25, 1952.

Lauren Tarshis, "The German Giant," *Scholastic Update*, January 24, 1992.

"Text of Protest on Curbs in Germany," *The New York Times,* May 31, 1952.

Terry Tillman, *The Writings on the Wall*. Santa Monica, CA: 22/7 Publishing Co., 1990.

Jo Ann Tooley, "Family Reunion," *U.S. News & World Report*, October 8, 1990.

Denise M. Topolnicki, "Laughing at Their Family's Fate," *Money*, October 1991.

Melanie Wallace et al., "Struggling to Define Democracy," *Scholastic Update*, March 9, 1990.

Russell Watson et al., "A Society Deep in Crisis," *Newsweek*, November 20, 1989.

Benjamin Welles, "Churchill Likens Berlin to Munich," *The New York Times*, June 27, 1948.

Adam Zagorin, "On Each Other's Nerves," *Time*, September 28, 1992.

Index

abortion, 82
Adenauer, Konrad, 23
  first FRG chancellor, 15-16
Albrecht, Hans, 79
Alliance 90, 50
Allies (World War II)
  end-of-war objectives for
    Germany, 11-12
  Soviet Union and strained relations,
    12-13
anti-Semitism
  problems after reunification, 98-101
Arbed S.A. company, 66
asyl (political asylum), 95
athletic programs
  government-sponsored in GDR, 92

BASF company, 66
Basic Law
  constitution of FRG, 15
Bayer company, 66
Berlin Wall
  as *Schandmauer* (Wall of Shame), 25
  built, 23
  east-to-west escapes
    before Wall, 20-23
    despite Wall, 24-25
  symbol of Communism, 25
  Wall falls, 7, 36-37
Biedenkopf, Kurt, 60-61
Bismarck, Otto von, 8
Bohley, Barbel, 90
Brandenburg Gate, 98
Brandt, Willy, 27
Breuel, Birgit, 64-65, 112
Brezhnev, Leonid, 80
Bridge of Unification, 114
Britain
  concerns about reunification, 51

Two-Plus-Four and, 52

Charlemagne (Charles the Great), 8
Christian Democratic Union, 15, 42,
  44, 75, 112
Christian Social Union, 15, 75
Churchill, Winston, 13-14
Coca-Cola Company, 66
collectivized farms, 28
Committee to Dissolve the National
  Security, 76
Communism
  history of, 17
  ruling force in GDR, 17-19
  Stasi and Communist crimes, 19, 50,
    76-81

Daimler-Benz company, 66
de Maiziere, Lothar, 50-51, 77
Democracy Now party, 50
Democratic Awakening party, 79
Democratic Socialist party, 112
Deutsche Bundesbank, 84
deutsche mark (DM)
  introduction of, 13
  deutsche-mark millionaires, 28
Droschler, Eve, 42

eastern Germany after reunification
  big businesses move in, 65-66
  defense reorganization, 83-84
  differing values, 87-89
  economic outlook, 109-12
  exodus to west continues, 59-61
  financial mismanagement, 92-94
  frustration at changes, 90-92
  hardships of unification, 56-59
    unemployment, 9, 56-58, 106
  new identity and self-esteem, 101-3

political outlook, 112-13
pollution and costs of reform, 47-49
private investment needed, 63-65
progress, slow, 68-69
scandal during reunification, 50-52
scorn by the West, 89-90
social and fiscal reform, 49
social outlook, 113-15
unemployment, 9, 56-58, 106
East Germany
See German Democratic Republic
(GDR)
EC
See European Community
educational reform
political issue, 83
EEC
See European Economic Community
Environmental Union, 48
Erhard, Ludwig, 16
European Community (EC), 51, 84, 85
European Economic Community
(EEC), 27

Fechter, Peter, 25
Federal Republic of Germany (FRG),
7
Basic Law (constitution), 15
established, 14
organizational structure, 15-16
pact with GDR, 27
prosperity and good life, 28-29
reunification with East Germany, 7,
8-9
strain from eastern exodus, 34-35
see also Berlin Wall; western
Germany after reunification
Fink, Heinrich, 78-79
Fischer, Werner, 76
France
anxiety about German reunification,
43
concerns about reunification, 51
Two-Plus-Four and, 52
Free Democratic Party, 15
FRG
See Federal Republic of Germany
F.W. Woolworth stores, 67

GDR
See German Democratic Republic
GEMSU Treaty
environmental goals, 47-49
establishment, 45-46
social and fiscal reform, 49
Genscher, Hans-Dietrich, 52, 76,
84-85
German Communist Party, 18
German Democratic Republic (GDR),
8
athletic programs, 92
austerity and limited luxury, 28-30
constitution (in name only), 14,
16-17
elections, first actual (1990), 8, 44
"elections" under Communism, 19
established, 15
growing discontent under
Communism, 31
guaranteed employment and other
benefits, 28, 57
Jugendweihe ceremony, 103
Länder re-established, 49
organizational structure, theory
versus practice, 16-20
pact with FRG, 27
promises of reform, 35-36
reunification with West Germany, 7,
8-9
Stasi
problems, 19, 50
problems after reunification, 76-81
state-run economy, 19-20
see also Berlin Wall; eastern
Germany after unification
Gorbachev, Mikhail, 30-31, 32, 35
guaranteed employment in GDR, 28,
57
Gysi, Klaus, 101

Hanson, Edeltraud, 59
Hanson, Leonhard "Hardy", 58-59
Heine, Heinrich, 109
Henzler, Herbert, 105, 109-10
Holy Roman Empire, 8
Honecker, Erich, 28, 31-32, 35
trial and exile, 77, 78, 79, 80

Honecker, Margot, 32
Hungary
  easing of Communist yoke, 32
  refuge for West Germans, 33-34

Ilka company, 65
immigration
  problems after reunification, 95-98
Iron Curtain, 13
  holes in Curtain, 32-34, 36

Johnson, Lyndon, 23
Jugendweihe, 103

Kaiser, Gitta, 29-30
Kaiser, Janine, 29-30
Kaiser, Joachim, 29-30
Kessler, Heinz, 79
Kohl, Helmut
  estimated cost of unification, 62
  hero to villain, 69, 74-76
  plans for reunification, 38-39, 42, 55
  reunification problems continue, 81,
    85, 98
  unification chancellor, 71-72
Krenz, Egon, 35-36
Kruse, Martin, 115
Kurfürstendamm, 37

Länder (states)
  of FRG, 16
  of GDR re-established, 49
Lenin, Vladimir, 17

McDonald's restaurants, 66
Marx, Karl, 17
Mazowiecki, Tadeusz, 31
Meckel, Markus, 41
Mercedes democracy, 73
Mielke, Erich, 77, 78
Ministry of State Security
  See Stasi
Möllemann, Jürgen, 38-39, 42, 55

Nationalist Front, 97
NATO
  See North Atlantic Treaty
    Organization

neo-Nazis (skinheads), 99, 108
New Forum party, 50, 90
New York Times, 16
Nicholas II
  czar of Russia, 17
North Atlantic Treaty Organization
  (NATO), 27, 51-52
Nuremberg Trials, 12, 81

Opel company, 66
Ossis, 89
Ostmark
  introduced, 13
  replaced, 46

Perestroika, 30-31
Petermann, Simon, 84
Pieck, Wilhelm, 17-18
Poland
  anxiety about German reunification,
    43
  discontent with Communism, 30
  relief from totalitarian rule, 31
pollution
  GDR and, 47-49
Potte, Rainer, 114

Reber, Samuel, 21
Rohwedder, Detlev, 46
  assassinated, 64
Romania
  problems under Communism, 30

Sachsenhausen concentration camp,
  101
scandal
  during reunification, 50-52
Schandmauer (Wall of Shame), 25
Schmidt-Holtz, Rolf, 62
Schnabel, Claus, 69
Schnur, Wolfgang, 79
Seiters, Rudolf, 97
Shevardnadze, Eduard, 53
skinheads (neo-Nazis), 99, 108
Snyder, Louis, 18
Social Democratic party, 15, 75, 98
Socialist Unity party
  Communist party of GDR, 18

social outlook, 113-15
Solidarity
  political party in Poland, 30, 31
Soviet Union
  Allies and strained relations, 12-13
  blockade ended, 14
  blockade of Berlin, 13
  concerns about reunification, 51
  established East Germany as puppet
    state, 13
  Two-Plus-Four and, 52
Stalin, Joseph, 17
Stasi (secret police), 19, 50
  investigation and prosecution, 76-81
Stoltenberg, Gerhard, 75-76
Stoph, Willi, 79
Streletz, Franz, 79
suicide rates
  reunification and, 95

Technische Gummiwaren company,
  67-68
Tittman, Karin, 37
*Treaty on the Final Settlement with
  Respect to Germany*, 52-53
Treuhand (Trust Fund Institution)
  closure of businesses, 57, 107
  criticism of, 49-50
  establishment of, 45-46
  wrapped in red tape, 64
Trust Fund Institution
  See Treuhand
Two-Plus-Four conference, 52-53

Ulbricht, Walter, 18-20, 31
unemployment
  East Germany after unification, 9,
    56-58, 106
United States
  concerns about reunification, 51
  Two-Plus-Four and, 52
unity bonds, 45

Volkswagen company, 66

Waigel, Theo, 61
Wall of Shame (*Schandmauer*), 25
Warsaw Pact, 27, 51

Wessis, 89-90, 101
western Germany after reunification
  anti-Semitism, again, 98-101
  big business goes east, 65-66
  costs of reunification
    estimated, 44-45
    realistic, 55
  differing values, 87-89
  domestic issues, 81-83
  immigration problems, 95-98
  sacrifice necessary, 61-62
  Stasi problems, 76-81
  strikes in protest, 62-63
  taxes and discontent, 9, 62
  Treuhand's problems, 64-65
West Germany
  See Federal Republic of Germany
    (FRG)
Wolffsohn, Michael, 81
Wollenberger, Knud, 79

xenophobia, 96

Zack, Michael, 67-68

About the Author

Diane Yancey began writing for her own entertainment when she was a thirteen-year-old living in Grass Valley, California. Later, she graduated from Augustana College in Illinois. She now pursues a writing career in the Pacific Northwest, where she lives with her husband, two daughters, and two cats. Her interests include collecting old books, building miniature houses, and traveling.

Ms. Yancey's first book, *Desperadoes and Dynamite*, deals with the colorful people and events surrounding train robbery in the United States. Besides *The Reunification of Germany*, she has also written a book of medical mysteries and a book on the U.S. Camel Corps.

Picture Credits

Cover Photo: AP/Wide World Photos
AP/Wide World Photos, 9, 18 (top), 33, 35 (top), 43, 51, 54, 56, 58, 60, 61 (both), 64, 72, 74, 75, 78, 86, 93, 107
The Bettmann Archive, 8, 17 (both)
© Regis Bossu/Sygma, 67, 104, 110, 111, 114
© Henning Christoph, Fotoarchiv, Black Star, 48
National Archives, 12
© T. Raupach/Argus, 44, 45
© Thomas Raupach/Argus/Focus, 88
Reuters/Bettmann, 6, 26, 29, 31, 32 (both), 34, 35 (bottom), 37, 38, 39, 40, 47, 52, 63, 70, 77, 79, 80, 81, 82, 97, 98, 99, 100, 101, 108, 113
© A. Tannenbaum/Sygma, 106
UPI/Bettmann, 10, 13, 14 (both), 16, 18 (bottom), 20, 21 (both), 22, 23, 24, 30